HUMAN RIGHTS AS
POLITICS
AND IDOLATRY

THE UNIVERSITY CENTER
FOR HUMAN VALUES SERIES

AMY GUTMANN AND STEPHEN MACEDO, EDITORS

3

Human Rights as Politics and Idolatry

❖ MICHAEL IGNATIEFF ❖

K. ANTHONY APPIAH

DAVID A. HOLLINGER

THOMAS W. LAQUEUR

DIANE F. ORENTLICHER

EDITED AND INTRODUCED BY

AMY GUTMANN

PRINCETON UNIVERSITY PRESS

PRINCETON AND OXFORD

Copyright © 2001 by Princeton University Press
Published by Princeton University Press, 41 William Street,
Princeton, New Jersey 08540
In the United Kingdom: Princeton University Press, 3 Market Place,
Woodstock, Oxfordshire OX20 1SY

All Rights Reserved

Third printing, and first paperback printing, 2003
Paperback ISBN 0-691-11474-9

The Library of Congress has cataloged the cloth edition of this book as follows

Ignatieff, Michael.
Human rights as politics and idolatry / Michael Ignatieff ; edited and
introduced by Amy Gutmann.
p. cm. — (University Center for Human Values series)
Includes bibliographical references and index.
ISBN 0-691-08893-4 (alk. paper)
1. Human rights. 2. Political science—Philosophy. 3. World
politics. I. Gutmann, Amy. II. Title. III. Series.

JC571 .I39 2001
323—dc21   2001032102

British Library Cataloging-in-Publication Data is available

This book has been composed in Baskerville

Printed on acid-free paper. ∞

www.pupress.princeton.edu

Printed in the United States of America

7   9   10   8

ISBN-13: 978-0-691-11474-3 (pbk.)

CONTENTS

Introduction

AMY GUTMANN

"No ONE shall be subject to cruel, inhuman, or degrading treatment or punishment." This statement of Article 7 of the International Covenant on Civil and Political Rights is part of what Michael Ignatieff aptly calls "the juridical revolution" in human rights since 1945. Other critical international documents of the revolution include the Universal Declaration of Human Rights and the Geneva Conventions of 1948, the revision of the Geneva Conventions of 1949, and the international convention on asylum of 1951.

Covenants without swords are but words, Thomas Hobbes famously wrote. What kind of revolution is marked by so many words that lack the backing of swords? The International Covenant, unlike the original Universal Declaration, is a legally binding treaty among nations. A Human Rights Committee has the authority to adjudicate violations that are brought before it. The legally binding nature of this and other human rights treaties is another indication of the rights revolution. To say that human rights are legally binding, however, is not to say that there is an authoritative agent with the power to hold sovereign states to the law. For this and many other reasons, the human rights revolution is far from complete, and its capacity to come closer to realizing its aims is widely questioned, especially outside of now highly organized communities of human rights activists. Moreover, what would count as a successful completion of the human rights revolution is by no means clear, or clearly established in either the theory or the practice of human rights in the international arena.

We therefore begin this book with the most basic set of questions concerning the political morality of human rights. What is the purpose of human rights? What should their content be? When do violations of human rights warrant intervention across national boundaries? Is there a single moral foundation for human rights that spans many cultures, or are there many culturally specific moral foundations, or none? In what sense, if any, are human rights universal? These are among the hard and critical questions raised by the human rights revolution, and addressed by Michael Ignatieff's two essays in this volume and the commentaries by Anthony Appiah, David Hollinger, Thomas Laqueur, and Diane Orentlicher to which Ignatieff responds. The essays and commentaries were first presented as the 1999–2000 Tanner Lectures on Human Values at Princeton University under the auspices of Princeton's University Center for Human Values.

If we begin with the most basic question—What is the purpose of human rights?—we will immediately see how hard it is to arrive at a meeting of minds on a single answer. Harder to see, apparently, is how unnecessary it is to insist on a single answer. Human rights can serve multiple purposes, and those purposes can be expressed in many ways, not only across different societies and cultures, but even within them. No major culture is univocal in its answer to this question. That there can be many good answers to a single question as practically important as the purpose of human rights should not prevent us from offering our own best answer, especially if that answer is one that speaks to many people, as does Ignatieff's understanding of human rights.

The purpose of human rights, Ignatieff argues, is to protect human agency and therefore to protect human agents against abuse and oppression. Human rights protect the core of negative freedom, freedom from abuse, oppression, and cruelty. This is a starting point for some complex thinking about what the purpose and content of the evolving international human rights regime should be. But even the starting point is more complex—and contestable—than first appearances might suggest. Protecting human agencies, and protecting human agents against abuse and oppression, cannot be identified simply (or solely) with negative liberty, freedom *from* interference. Nor is the core of human rights constituted only by negative freedoms. The right to subsistence is as necessary for human agency as a right against torture. A right to subsistence is not a negative freedom, as the right against cruel and unusual punishment is. Starving people have no more agency than people subject to cruel and unusual punishment. Including subsistence rights in the human rights regime was also an important part of reaching an international agreement on the nature of human rights.

If an important purpose of human rights is to protect human agency, and the rights that protect human agency are not exclusively negative liberties, it is still the case, as Ignatieff argues, that a human rights regime does not claim—or realistically aspire—to be morally comprehensive. The enforcement of human rights in the international arena does not guarantee that anyone whose rights are effectively protected will live a wonderful life. Or even a (morally or nonmorally) good life. When human rights are honored and enforced, they are effective instruments to protect individuals from abuse, cruelty, oppression, degradation, and the like. This purpose of human rights—which Ignatieff calls pragmatic, which is not to deny that it is moral in its core purpose of protecting human agency (just as pragmatism is a moral and political philosophy)—can provide a guide to the content of a human rights regime. Human rights institutions and agencies—both governmental and nongovernmental—should not try to proliferate human rights beyond what is necessary to protect persons as purposive agents, or to realize a similarly basic purpose of human rights (such as the dignity of persons, a purpose that Ignatieff rejects and to which I shall return). Proliferation of human rights to include rights that are not clearly necessary to protect the basic agency or needs or dignity of persons cheapens the purpose of human rights and correspondingly weakens the resolve of potential enforcers.

Proliferation of human rights also makes it far more difficult to achieve the broad intercultural assent to rights that an international human rights regime requires to be effective. If human rights are pragmatic political instruments, then human rights regimes should aspire to be effective before they aspire to be more comprehensive in their pronouncements. Human rights should not be conceived as guarantors of social justice, or substitutes for comprehensive conceptions of a good life. Protections against cruel, inhuman, and degrading treatment—all of which are compatible with multiple expressions of the purpose of human rights—are widely viewed as the core of a human rights regime. If protections against cruelty and degradation—freedom from harm and freedom to live a decent life—are not human rights, then one might say that nothing is. And some people, of course, do say that nothing is a human right, but that does not mean that they are right, or even reasonable in claiming that there are no human rights. To believe in human rights does not entail believing that they exist independently of human purpose. Human rights are important instruments for protecting human beings against cruelty, oppression, and degradation. That's all we need to believe to defend human rights. Many people believe far more about human rights, for example, that there is a divine or natural source of human rights. The human purpose of defending human rights, however, may not differ dramatically, even if the imputed sources do.

But must a human rights regime be restricted (or restrict itself) to protections of negative freedoms alone to be effective, to gain international assent and enforcement, as Ignatieff sometimes suggests? I am doubtful in light of the arguments (including many made by Ignatieff himself), the evidence of the origins of the Universal Declaration, and the apparent need to include rights to subsistence (which are not negative freedoms) to gain international assent to most human rights documents in the global arena. Although rights to subsistence and to basic political freedoms (due process, habeas corpus) are not negative liberties, they too are a necessary part of what it means to treat people as purposive agents, and to protect them against degrading treatment, of which dire poverty is certainly one form. A human rights regime still needs to avoid overextending itself beyond what are reasonable aspirations. But it also needs to avoid a minimalism so sparing that its enforcement would leave the most vulnerable people without what is (minimally) necessary to protect their ability to live a minimally decent life by any reasonable standards. Starving people are denied their human agency. They are also being denied their dignity, and they are being degraded. They are not being treated as agents with a human life to lead. There are many other ways to describe the gross injustice inflicted upon starving people in today's world, where there are ways both to prevent starvation and to address it when it occurs. What counts as minimal human rights is bound to be contentious, and broad assent is essential for effective enforcement. But there is good reason to think that an effective human rights regime needs to safeguard subsistence rights as well as a set of negative liberties.

Another reason to wonder whether we should hold human rights regimes to only the most minimalist standards is that problems of agreement, interpretation, and enforcement inhere even in the most minimalist formulations of human rights. "Minimal" is not necessarily synonymous with "maximally consensual" or "easiest to enforce." It may be easier to enlist agreement on a set of human rights that combine protections of negative freedoms with subsistence, and maybe even other welfare rights, than it is to insist on restricting a human rights regime to negative liberties alone. Ignatieff makes no such insistence, but he often argues or alludes to the idea that human agency supports only negative liberty. I have argued that human agency itself supports more than negative liberty. But my argument is only one of several that could be cited in defense of subsistence rights (and perhaps also more rights) as part of a human rights regime that is neither minimalist nor maximalist.

Despite the attraction of minimalism, it must be said that what counts as a minimal set of human rights is by no means either obvious or agreed upon by even good-willed people. Even the means of protecting people against "cruel, inhuman, or degrading . . . punishment" is open to reasonable disagreement. When the Taliban stone women to death for adultery, this is about as clear a violation of a human right against cruel, inhuman, and degrading treatment as any. But does the United States violate a human right that belongs in the minimal set when its judicial system sentences people to death? Does capital punishment as practiced today in the United States constitute a human rights violation under Article 7? To answer in the affirmative, one need not think that capital punishment is equivalent to the worst atrocities committed by the Taliban. To answer in the negative, one need not approve of capital punishment or even be anything less than an ardent opponent of the practice. This example illustrates the problem of determining how to characterize even a minimal set of human rights. If capital punishment violates a minimal set of human rights, then it cannot be said that the minimal set is uncontroversial, or that it lends itself to effective international enforcement. The U.S. government is famous—or infamous, depending on one's perspective—for not acknowledging the legitimacy of human rights enforcement against its own authority on grounds that its authority is rooted in the "consent of the governed" to constitutional democratic sovereignty. The example of capital punishment reveals that the sovereignty of a constitutional democratic regime is no guarantee against tyranny of the majority or minority. (Majorities often do not rule in democracies.) It also remains an open question as to whether more than minimal human rights—an avidly moderate regime of human rights—would fare better or worse by way of international agreement and enforcement.

An equally serious problem for human rights in the international arena—illustrated by the self-exemption of many societies from all or part of the human rights regime—is nationalism. Nationalism is often asserted as a human rights claim on behalf of a self-determining "people." Ignatieff perceptively argues that nationalism is a double-edged sword. Universalized as a human right, nationalism is conceived as the right of collective self-determination. This raises the question of whether collective self-determination is part of the minimal set of human rights because it is intrinsically valuable (for a self-determining "people") or because it is an instrument, a means (as human rights should be) for protecting individuals who share a society together against the worst cruelties that politically organized societies can inflict on individuals. The idea that secure states can better guarantee rights than any available alternative is an instrumental defense of collective self-determination, but not a defense of nationalism per se. To defend collective self-determination as a right that is instrumental to protecting individuals against cruelty, one need not believe that every "people" has a right to its own self-determining society, which would permit it to exercise sovereignty over its members. When a right to collective self-determination is identified with a defense of nationalism, understood as the self-determination of a people, the right loses its clear connection to protection of human agency against cruelty, oppression, and degradation. This is because, as Ignatieff recognizes, "nationalism solves the human rights problems of the victorious national groups while producing new victim groups, whose human rights situation is made worse." Collective self-determination needs to be distinguished from nationalism for it to qualify as a means of protecting all persons against the worst forms of cruelty and oppression. There is no right to victimize individuals in the name of being a people or nation. Nationalism is the response to one human rights problem and the creation of another because nations assume the authority to victimize individuals under the guise of their right to self-determination.

A human rights regime therefore cannot consistently defend nationalism—or the absolute sovereignty of a people—as what the human right of collective self-determination entails. Collective self-determination as a human right does not carry with it the authority to oppress minorities. Collective self-determination is a human right exercised in groups, which is conditional—as are all such group rights—on the group's respecting the other rights of individuals. Whenever collective self-determination is confused with national sovereignty in an unqualified sense, it increases the risk of other rights violations; indeed, it sometimes supports other rights violations. Human rights violations cannot be justified—or even condoned or excused—in the name of nationalism; human rights violations render nationalistic states "subject to criticism, sanction, and, as a final resort, intervention." Determining that a nation-state has violated basic human rights, however, does not tell us whether and what kind of criticism, sanction, or intervention is likely to succeed in improving the situation of oppressed individuals, which is, of course, the purpose of human rights as political instruments.

The most controversial—and sometimes the only potentially effective—response to persistent human rights violations by states is intervention. Under what conditions, Ignatieff therefore asks, is intervention justified to reverse human rights abuses within states? Like nationalism, intervention is a double-edged sword. It must be used sparingly lest it become an unintended excuse for human rights violations on the part of intervening states. Yet it must be used when it can be effective to stop (or at least significantly reduce) systematic and pervasive human rights abuses. This standard is far harder to apply than it is to articulate, and it is controversial in both theory and application. "Human rights may be universal, but support for coercive enforcement of their norms will never be universal." If this is realism, it is no recipe for isolationism. The failure to intervene in Rwanda, for example, where many lives could have been saved, was far from inevitable or justifiable. Such failures have "undermined the credibility of human rights values in zones of danger around the world."

Arguments about when states should intervene to vindicate human rights are controversial for the obvious reason that so much is at stake in any decision about intervention. But human rights are also highly controversial when what is at stake is in no way obvious. What, pragmatically minded people might ask with some incredulity, is at stake in the equally heated—and quite common— arguments about the metaphysical and moral foundations of human rights? These arguments—for example, about human agency, dignity, and natural law—tend to be quite abstract, and it may therefore be tempting to assume that not much of practical importance is at stake. But such an assumption would be rash. What is at stake in determining the foundations of human rights is often the very legitimacy of human rights talk in the international arena. If human rights necessarily rest on a moral or metaphysical foundation that is not in any meaningful sense universal or publicly defensible in the international arena, if human rights are based on exclusively Eurocentric ideas, as many critics have (quite persistently) claimed, and these Eurocentric ideas are biased against non-Western countries and cultures, then the political legitimacy of human rights talk, human rights covenants, and human rights enforcement is called into question.

"People may not agree why we have rights," Ignatieff writes, "but they can agree that they need them." On what is this agreement based? According to Ignatieff, people can agree that we all need human rights because without human rights individuals lack "agency." I am less sure that people can all agree that we need human rights on the basis of the need for human "agency." My uncertainty does not stem from disagreeing with Ignatieff that human agency is a strong basis for human rights. I heartily agree and would be happy to defend the claim on both moral and pragmatic grounds (pragmatic grounds in this realm turn out also to be moral, and not coincidentally so). My disagreement with Ignatieff is over whether a human rights regime rests on a single foundation—the one agreeable to all, or to most people—or on several foundations, no one of which is likely to be agreeable to most people. The several foundations of human rights, taken together, are likely to be agreeable to more people than any single foundation, and no single foundation has a monopoly on reasonable claims to be made in its favor.

There is also reason to doubt that human rights as pragmatic instruments in an international human rights regime can do without foundations altogether. Ignatieff sometimes speaks as if his own candidate for the reason for defending human rights—human agency—is not a foundation but something else, perhaps a more pragmatic idea. But human agency is a kind of foundation for human rights, even if not the kind of foundation that many people may think is philosophically necessary for something as highly valued as a human right. If we have human rights to protect human agency, then we may have an undefeatable reason to defend human rights, and that is all a philosophical foundation needs to be: a reason that is so good it is undefeatable (at least given what we now know). Nor is this reason in the least bit trivial or uncontroversial. To say that human rights are needed for human agency is to say something nontrivial about "why we have rights." We have rights because we are purposive agents who should be treated as such by our fellow human beings. The idea that we are purposive agents who are self-originating sources of claims is quite controversial. Human rights are more easily defended in some cultures by claims about human dignity, or the respect owed to human beings, or the equal creation of human beings, than by the notion of human agency as a source of value in the world. (The idea of human agency can support human rights only if human agency itself is thought to be valuable and therefore worth protecting.)

To avoid the kinds of philosophical controversies that rage over what the right foundation is for human rights, Ignatieff wants to forgo foundational arguments rooted in human dignity, natural law, divine creative purpose, and related notions. Human agency, however, is a related notion, and that is part of its strength as a guide to what should count as a human right. If human agency were not related to human dignity, for example, it would be less well suited to supporting the weight of human rights recognition and enforcement. The alternative to eschewing any foundational argument is to encourage human rights regimes to rely on many foundational arguments. The reason Ignatieff wants to avoid foundational arguments is a good one: "A universal regime of human rights protection ought to be compatible with moral pluralism." It does not follow that a regime of human rights should deny any foundation. Far better—for both moral and pragmatic reasons—that it rely on many foundational arguments. A human rights regime that welcomes an overlapping consensus is more compatible with moral pluralism. It is also more compatible with respect for the many cultural and philosophical traditions that converge in support of a similar set of human rights. This convergence is not complete or perfect, but neither is the convergence on human rights from *within* a single cultural or philosophical tradition.

To say that a universal regime of human rights should be compatible with moral pluralism is not to say that it must be compatible with every belief system. Human rights cannot be so indiscriminately embracing of every existing belief system, or at least not of every dominant interpretation of every existing belief system. The dominant belief system of the Taliban today denies the human agency of women, and their dignity, and it does so in manifest ways that are irreconcilable with any human rights regime. Perhaps the Taliban can be convinced to give up whatever beliefs they use to rationalize their oppression and abuse of women, but the failure to convince them to change their beliefs surely should not be taken as a challenge to the claim that human rights are universal in a meaningful sense, a sense that is often confused with the idea that human rights are universally accepted (which is clearly not the case). The meaningful sense in which human rights are universal is that they are morally defensible instruments even—or perhaps especially—in the face of oppressors who fail to recognize the human agency or dignity of those whose lives and liberties they are discounting. As Ignatieff puts it: "Rights are universal because they define the universal interests of the powerless."

What, then, does it mean to say that human rights protection is compatible with moral pluralism? A human rights regime that is compatible with moral pluralism must be consistent with a plurality of comprehensive belief systems. It need not be compatible with all such belief systems, since some fundamentally reject human rights. (As a terrifying example, one need only think of Nazi ideology.) But many belief systems accept the need for human rights, and the plural sources of support for human rights were in evidence at the origins of the juridical rights revolution. The drafting of the Universal Declaration of Human Rights involved people tied to cultural traditions in North and South America, Europe, Asia, and Africa, and religious traditions including Islam, Judaism, Eastern and Western Christianity, Hinduism, and more. Since the time of the drafting of the first documents, the evidence has only increased on the side of the idea that many cultures can converge in support of human rights.

Why, then, do we pay any heed to the idea that human rights are parochial? Because from the time of the drafting, the evidence has also been overwhelming that many members of these and other cultures and religions adamantly oppose some of the most basic human rights— along with the very idea that human rights are essential for protecting *individual agency* or *human dignity* as distinct from *the survival of the collectivity*. What human rights protection seeks is not the destruction of cultures, as critics too often accuse, but their integration of human rights protection, as critics too often deny is possible. The critics' prophecy that human rights will destroy their culture can be self-fulfilling—by encouraging resistance against human rights recognition—but it is not inevitable that this resistance result in either the culture's destruction or the ongoing oppression of powerless people. Oppressed women typically want their rights as individuals to be secured within their own culture, not at the expense of exile from their culture, or the destruction of what they and others take to be valuable about their culture. All cultures that have arisen in the midst of quite perva-

sive human rights violations—as most cultures have—
must change in order to honor the most basic human
rights of women and vulnerable minorities. When cultures and societies accommodate the human rights of
women, they do not cease to exist; they change, often
quite dramatically, in ways that are morally and politically
significant.

Ignatieff commends the mother document of the human rights revolution, the Universal Declaration, for
avoiding contentious religious grounds for human rights
and instead offering a secular ground, which is "a pragmatic common denominator designed to make agreement possible across the range of divergent cultural and
political viewpoints." The secular ground that Ignatieff
defends is a recognition of the importance of human
agency. The grounding of human rights in a defense of
human agency is widely acceptable across many cultures.
But I have offered some reasons to think that it is not
necessary that any *single* grounding be acceptable to all
supporters, whether the grounding be human agency or
some other secular or religious conception of what makes
human rights important. What a human rights regime re-
lies on, instead, are plural foundations, no one of which
needs to be authoritative to all human rights defenders.
Plural foundations make a human rights regime more
broadly acceptable to people.

Do plural foundations make a human rights regime
philosophically or morally incoherent? Not at all. A human rights regime is a political instrument, and as such it
should have foundations that suit its purpose. When international groups publicly respect a plurality of grounds,
rather than insisting on only one or no ground, human

rights are publicly defended for a plurality of reasons as a recognized part of what it means for a pluralistic world to support an international human rights regime. If there are many reasonable grounds of human rights, rather than just one (or none), then there is a good reason for political morality to recommend that official international documents eschew any assertion of "the" proper metaphysical foundation of human rights. At the same time, there is also good reason for a human rights regime to welcome a plurality of nonexclusive claims concerning the ways in which human rights can legitimately be grounded, in religious and secular claims of various sorts. Human agency, the dignity of human beings, and equal creation are three of the several foundations that are not mutually exclusive, although advocates of different moral foundations often treat the foundations as more important to honor than the rights themselves. When foundations are treated as more important to honor than the rights themselves, and disagreement about foundations becomes a cause for violating rights, then "idolatry" of abstract ideas, quite apart from the practical consequences of such idolatry, becomes a serious political problem. Having the right foundational faith should not be treated as more important than treating individuals decently by actually honoring their rights.

To respect human agency or dignity, one might argue, entails respecting (even if not accepting) a wide range of reasonable views about the foundations of human rights. After all, free people are likely to disagree more about metaphysical foundations than we do about far more consequential claims, upon which many of our divergent foundational claims (not coincidentally) converge. The foundations of utilitarianism and deontology are as dramatically different as are the foundations of many religious and secular belief systems. But different foundations need not prevent convergence in defense of a set of basic human rights. This is true even with regard to communitarian philosophies, many of which can and do defend human rights, albeit from a metaphysical perspective that is at odds with liberal individualism. However, communitarian defenses of human rights do not deny the moral worth of individuals; they instead defend a closer constitutive connection between individuals and communities than do many liberals. An absolute and unwavering denial of the moral worth of individuals is incompatible with a defense of human rights. But in most cases where people continue to reasonably disagree, they also profit from deliberative engagement and argument—without fear of persecution—that human rights also make possible.

A defense of human rights as pragmatic instruments raises the question of whether an international human rights regime can do without all moral and metaphysical foundations by defending itself on pragmatic grounds. Ignatieff is tempted to argue that it can and should, while his commentators are dubious about whether it can or should. But does Ignatieff really defend doing without moral and metaphysical foundations? I don't think so. Ignatieff cites Article 1 of the Universal Declaration as a model of how the human rights regime gets along well without moral and metaphysical justification. But does Article 1 really do without mentioning any moral or metaphysical foundations? Let's consider what Article 1 declares:

All human beings are born free and equal in dignity and rights. They are endowed with reason and conscience and should act towards one another in a spirit of brotherhood.

In these two simple sentences, the Declaration does not assert a single foundation for human rights. But neither does it eschew all foundations. Instead, it briefly declares many foundations:

- Free and equal personhood: "All human beings are born free and equal"
- Equal dignity: "free and equal in dignity"
- Equal creation or endowment: "They are endowed with reason and conscience"
- Equal brotherhood: "a spirit of brotherhood"
- Human agency: "endowed with reason and conscience"

Each of these allusions to foundations is also open to multiple interpretations. In keeping with the idea that human rights can be defended on a plurality of grounds, these two sentences point not to a single foundation for human rights but to several.

To say that human rights have foundations, however, is not to say that our attitude toward them, or toward the human beings who are their subjects, should be worshipful, or in any other way reverential, let alone idolatrous. To respect human beings is not to worship them—or to worship human rights in a way that does not permit any compromises in the enforcement of some human rights for the sake of protecting others, or for the sake of the social conditions that are prerequisite to the protection of any human rights. This worry about worshiping human rights rather than valuing the lives of the people who are supposed to be protected by human rights raises the question of how we can respect our fellow human beings without treating rights with a reverential attitude. "With the idea of rights," Ignatieff writes, "goes a commitment to respect the reasoned commitments of others and to submit disputes to adjudication." Ignatieff's view of human rights as protecting human agency supports this commitment to deliberating about our disagreements.

Ignatieff defends toleration rather than respect as a fundamental commitment of a human rights regime. I am less sure than he that a human rights regime can do without at least a minimal commitment to respect as well as toleration. Ignatieff connects his commitment to deliberation about our disagreements to toleration rather than respect: "The fundamental moral commitment entailed by rights is not to respect, and certainly not to worship. It is to deliberation." I suspect that a willingness to deliberate with people with whom we disagree—as distinct from a willingness simply to let them be—depends on more than toleration only. I suspect that it also depends on our respect for them as agents with whom we can productively engage in argument. To tolerate but not respect others is "to live and let live," to restrain ourselves from interfering with their freedom to live their own lives as they (and not we) see fit. Toleration prevents us from interfering in other people's lives as long as they do not harm others. Toleration is a very good thing in human affairs. But it is not the only good thing. And it is not enough in the realm of human rights precisely because we cannot agree once and for all on what a human rights regime should include. We therefore depend for progress in the realm of human rights—as in so many other political realms—on deliberation as well as toleration. And to deliberate with other people, we need to do more than tolerate them; we need to engage with them constructively, which is itself a form of respect.

If we all could agree on what counts as not harming others, we might be able to settle for toleration in the sphere of international human rights. We would then not need to deliberate about the content of human rights. But as Ignatieff recognizes, we disagree, and deliberation is a way—a mutually respectful way—of trying to come closer to a reasoned agreement about human rights. Even when people who deliberate do not succeed in reaching agreement, they demonstrate some minimal degree of respect for one another by their efforts at deliberation.

A shared commitment to human rights might require no more than toleration were we already in agreement on the content of human rights. But since moral agents reasonably and passionately disagree, we may try to deliberate with one another in the hope of arriving at a better meeting of the minds and a more mutually justifiable meaning of human rights tomorrow than we have today. Deliberation therefore expresses more than an attitude of tolerance; it requires some minimal respect for people who have different, but reasonably thoughtful, views of human rights. A human rights regime tells us that we must tolerate unreasonable people, as long as they do not threaten to harm others. A commitment to deliberate with people with whom we disagree about human rights—in the hope of finding a better understanding tomorrow than we have today of our shared human rights regime—expresses respect for them, in the words of Article 1, as "endowed with reason and conscience." Respect for human dignity, agency, equality and freedom, brotherhood and sisterhood all are implied by Article 1. As it was drafted and has been interpreted since, Article 1 articulates not a single view but many broadly acceptable beginnings to an imperfect rights revolution whose end is not in sight.

HUMAN RIGHTS AS
POLITICS
AND IDOLATRY

MICHAEL IGNATIEFF

Human Rights as Politics

HUMAN RIGHTS AND MORAL PROGRESS

In *If This Is a Man,* Primo Levi describes being inter-
viewed by Dr. Pannwitz, chief of the chemical department
at Auschwitz.[1] Securing a place in the department was a
matter of life or death: if Levi could convince Pannwitz
that he was a competent chemist, he might be spared the
gas chamber. As Levi stood on one side of the doctor's
desk, in his concentration camp uniform, Dr. Pannwitz
stared up at him. Levi later remembered:

> That look was not one between two men; and if I
> had known how completely to explain the nature of
> that look, which came as if across the glass window of
> an aquarium between two beings who live in differ-
> ent worlds, I would also have explained the essence
> of the great insanity of the third German [reich].

Here was a scientist, trained in the traditions of European rational inquiry, turning a meeting between two human beings into an encounter between different species.

Progress may be a contested concept, but we make
progress to the degree that we act upon the moral intuition that Dr. Pannwitz was wrong: our species is one, and

Delivered as a Tanner Lecture on Human Values at Princeton University,
2000. Printed with permission of the Tanner Lectures on Human Values, a
Corporation, University of Utah, Salt Lake City, Utah.

each of the individuals who compose it is entitled to equal moral consideration. Human rights is the language that systematically embodies this intuition, and to the degree that this intuition gains influence over the conduct of individuals and states, we can say that we are making moral progress. Richard Rorty's definition of progress applies here: "an increase in our ability to see more and more differences among people as morally irrelevant."[2] We think of the global diffusion of this idea as progress for two reasons: because if we live by it, we treat more human beings as we would wish to be treated ourselves, and in so doing help to reduce the amount of cruelty and unmerited suffering in the world. Our grounds for believing that the spread of human rights represents moral progress, in other words, are pragmatic and historical. We know from historical experience that when human beings have defensible rights—when their agency as individuals is protected and enhanced—they are less likely to be abused and oppressed. On these grounds, we count the diffusion of human rights instruments as progress even if there remains an unconscionable gap between the instruments and the actual practices of states charged to comply with them.

Calling the global diffusion of Western human rights a sign of moral progress may seem Eurocentric. Yet the human rights instruments created after 1945 were not a triumphant expression of European imperial self-confidence but a war-weary generation's reflection on European nihilism and its consequences. Human rights was a response to Dr. Pannwitz, to the discovery of the abomination that could occur when the Westphalian state was accorded unlimited sovereignty, when citizens of that state lacked normative grounds to disobey legal but immoral orders. The Universal Declaration of Human Rights represented a return by the European tradition to its natural law heritage, a return intended to restore *agency*, to give individuals the civic courage to stand up when the state ordered them to do wrong.

THE JURIDICAL, ADVOCACY, AND ENFORCEMENT REVOLUTIONS

Historically speaking, the Universal Declaration is part of a wider reordering of the normative order of postwar international relations, designed to create fire walls against barbarism. The juridical revolution included the UN Charter of 1945, outlawing aggressive war between states; the Genocide Convention of 1948, protecting religious, racial, and ethnic groups against extermination; the revision of the Geneva Conventions of 1949, strengthening noncombatant immunity; and finally the international convention on asylum of 1951 to protect the rights of refugees.

Before the Second World War, only states had rights in international law. With the Universal Declaration of Human Rights of 1948, the rights of individuals received international legal recognition.[3] For the first time, individuals—regardless of race, creed, gender, age, or any other status—were granted rights that they could use to challenge unjust state law or oppressive customary practice.

The international rights revolution was not led by states that already practiced what they preached. America and the European nations had not completed the juridical emancipation of their own citizens or subject peoples.

Indeed, many of the states that contributed to the drafting of the Universal Declaration saw no apparent contradiction between endorsing international norms abroad and continuing oppression at home. They thought that the Universal Declaration would remain a pious set of clichés more practiced in the breach than in the observance. Yet once articulated as international norms, rights language ignited both the colonial revolutions abroad and the civil rights revolution at home. The juridical revolution should not be seen apart from the struggle for self-determination and national independence among the colonies of Europe's empires and, just as important, the battle for full civil rights by black Americans, culminating in the Civil Rights Act of 1965.[4]

Fifty years on, most modern states have ratified the international human rights conventions, and some countries have incorporated their rights and remedies into the structure of their constitutions. The European Court of Human Rights, established in 1953, now affords citizens of European states the capacity to appeal against injustices in civil and state administration to the European Court in Strasbourg.[5] European states, including Britain, now accept that decisions taken by their courts or administrative bodies can be overturned by a human rights court independent of their national parliament and court systems.[6] New nations seeking entry into the European Union accept that they must align their domestic law in accordance with the European Convention, even jettisoning capital punishment, since it falls afoul of European human rights standards.

In the developing world, ratifying international human rights covenants has become a condition of entry for new states joining the family of nations. Even oppressive states feel obliged to engage in rhetorical deference toward human rights instruments. While genuflection toward human rights is the homage that vice pays to virtue, the fact that oppressive regimes feel so obliged means that vice can now be shamed and even controlled in ways that were unavailable before 1945.

The worldwide spread of human rights norms is often seen as a moral consequence of economic globalization. The U.S. State Department's annual report for 1999 on human rights practice around the world describes the constellation of human rights and democracy—along with "money and the Internet"—as one of the three universal languages of globalization.[7] This implies too easily that human rights is a style of moral individualism that has some elective affinity with the economic individualism of the global market, and that the two advance hand in hand. Actually, the relation between human rights and money, between moral and economic globalization, is more antagonistic, as can be seen, for example, in the campaigns by human rights activists against the labor and environmental practices of the large global corporations.[8] Human rights has gone global not because it serves the interests of the powerful but primarily because it has advanced the interests of the powerless. Human rights has gone global by going local, imbedding itself in the soil of cultures and worldviews independent of the West, in order to sustain ordinary people's struggles against unjust states and oppressive social practices.

We can call this global diffusion of human rights culture a form of moral progress even while remaining skeptical of the motives of those who helped to bring it about.

The states that signed the Universal Declaration never actually believed that it would constrain their behavior. After all, it lacked any enforcement mechanism. It was a declaration only, rather than a state treaty or a convention requiring national ratification. The drafters—men and women like Eleanor Roosevelt, René Cassin, and John Humphrey—were willing to live with a mere declaration because they believed that it would raise human rights consciousness around the world and in so doing restrain potential perpetrators of abuse.[9] We can respect their achievement while remaining skeptical about their faith. We have good reason to be doubtful about the preventive impact of human rights codes. Yet if human rights has not stopped the villains, it certainly has empowered bystanders and victims. Human rights instruments have given bystanders and witnesses a stake in abuse and oppression both within and beyond their borders, and this has called forth an advocacy revolution, the emergence of a network of nongovernmental human rights organizations—Amnesty International and Human Rights Watch being only the most famous—to pressure states to practice what they preach.[10] Because of this advocacy revolution, victims have gained historically unprecedented power to make their case known to the world.[11]

The advocacy revolution has broken the state's monopoly on the conduct of international affairs, enfranchising what has become known as global civil society. Here, too, we can believe in progress even while remaining dubious about the details. The phrase "global civil society" implies a cohesive moral movement when the reality is fierce and disputatious rivalry among nongovernmental organizations. These groups frequently claim that they represent human interests and human rights more effectively than governments, and while this is sometimes true, NGOs are not necessarily more representative or more accountable than *elected* governments. Global human rights consciousness, moreover, does not necessarily imply that the groups defending human rights actually believe the same things. Many of these NGOs espouse the universalist language of human rights but actually use it to defend highly particularist causes: the rights of particular national groups or minorities or classes of persons. There is nothing wrong with particularism in itself. Everyone's universalism ultimately anchors itself in a particular commitment to a specially important group of people whose cause is close to one's heart or convictions. The problem is that particularism conflicts with universalism at the point at which one's commitment to a group leads one to countenance human rights violations toward another group. Persons who care about human rights violations committed against Palestinians may not care so much about human rights violations committed by Palestinians against Israelis, and vice versa.

Human rights activism likes to portray itself as an antipolitics, in defense of universal moral claims designed to delegitimize "political" (i.e., ideological or sectarian) justifications for the abuse of human beings. In practice, impartiality and neutrality are just as impossible as universal and equal concern for everyone's human rights. Human rights activism means taking sides, mobilizing constituencies powerful enough to force abusers to stop. As a consequence, effective human rights activism is bound to be partial and political. Yet at the same time, human rights politics is disciplined or constrained by moral universals.

The role of moral universalism is not to take activists out of politics but to get activists to discipline their partiality—their conviction that one side is right—with an equal commitment to the rights of the other side.

Because human rights activists take it for granted that they represent universal values and universal interests, they have not always taken as much care as they might about the question of whether they truly represent the human interests they purport to defend. They are not elected by the victim groups they represent, and in the nature of things they cannot be. But this leaves unresolved their right to speak for and on behalf of the people whose rights they defend. A more acutely political, as opposed to moral activism might be more attentive to the question of whom activists represent and how far the right to represent extends. Few mechanisms of genuine accountability connect NGOs and the communities in civil society whose interests they seek to advance.[12]

Yet even if we grant that many NGOs are more particularist, and less accountable, than they claim, many others perform an essential function. By monitoring human rights abuses and bringing these abuses to light, they keep state signatories of human rights conventions up to the mark, or at least expose the gap between promise and practice, rhetoric and reality. Without the advocacy revolution of the NGOs, in other words, it is likely that the passage of so many human rights instruments since 1945 would have remained a revolution on paper.

Extraterritorial moral activism predates the Universal Declaration, of course. All human rights activism in the modern world properly traces its origins back to the campaigns to abolish the slave trade and then slavery itself.[13]

But the catastrophe of European war and genocide gave impetus to the ideal of moral intervention beyond national borders and to the proposition that a network of international activists could shame their own states into intervening in delinquent states in the name of universal values. Thanks to human rights advocacy, international politics has been democratized, and the pressure that human rights advocates can bring to bear on state actors—witness the campaigns on behalf of Soviet Jewry, or the international struggle against apartheid—has forced most states to accept that their foreign policy must at least pay rhetorical attention to values, as well as interests. Indeed, human rights considerations are now increasingly used to make the claim that in cases where values point one way and interests the other, values should trump. The United Nations system itself is beginning to reflect this new reality. Until the 1960s, UN bodies were wary of criticizing the human rights behavior of member states.[14] The apartheid regime of South Africa was the first exception, and after this breach in the wall there came others: the denunciation of the Greek junta in the 1970s, and the critique of repression in the Eastern bloc in the 1980s. After forty years of deference toward the sovereignty of states, the United Nations decided in the 1990s to create its own cadre of human rights activists under the leadership of the High Commissioner for Human Rights.[15] The commissioner's office still lacks financial resources and real support from UN member states, and the commissioner has the power only to name and shame defaulting governments. Still, every time a state is denounced for its human rights record, it becomes harder for it to secure international loans or political and military help when it is in danger. Naming and shaming for human rights abuses now have real consequences. Beyond the power to name and shame governments (and also private corporations) that violate human rights covenants, the international community has also created new instruments to punish violators. This is the enforcement revolution in human rights. The International Tribunal at Arusha secured the first convictions under the Genocide Convention since its promulgation in 1948. The prosecutors at The Hague have secured the first international convictions for war crimes since Nuremberg. The first international warrant for the arrest of a sitting head of state has been issued. The first forensic investigation of war crimes sites, immediately following a violation, was undertaken in Kosovo. These are important steps by any measure. The tribunal has done much to break the cycle of impunity in Rwanda, Bosnia, and now Kosovo. Each arrest of a suspect and each conviction by a tribunal help to substantiate the reality of a universal jurisdiction for crimes against humanity.[16] These tribunals, however, are temporary instruments created to respond to contingent catastrophes. The next step is the creation of a permanent International Criminal Tribunal. The statute for such a tribunal has been agreed on; and once ratified by a majority of states, it may finally be established, admittedly with its powers diluted and diminished, chiefly as a result of objections by the United States.

AMERICAN EXCEPTIONALISM

It is at this point, of course, that uncomfortable aspects of the human rights revolution reveal themselves, at least insofar as the United States is concerned. America's insistence on watering down the powers of the International Criminal Tribunal has opened up a significant rift with allies, like Britain and France, that can claim descent from the same family of rights traditions.[17] What bothers the American administration is not merely the prospect of seeing American military personnel brought before tendentious tribunals. Nor is American resistance to international human rights merely "rights narcissism"—the conviction that the land of Jefferson and Lincoln has nothing to learn from international rights norms.[18] It is that Americans believe their rights derive their legitimacy from their own consent, as embodied in the U.S. Constitution. International rights covenants lack this element of national political legitimacy.[19] Since the early 1950s, the American Congress has been reluctant to ratify international rights conventions. This ratification process—which, after all, is intended to vest these conventions with domestic political legitimacy—has often delayed full international implementation of the conventions or has introduced so many qualifications and reservations about American participation as to leave them enfeebled.

America's reluctant participation places it in a highly paradoxical relation to an emerging international legal order based on human rights principles. Since Eleanor Roosevelt chaired the committee that produced the Universal Declaration, America has promoted human rights norms around the world, while also resisting the idea that these norms apply to American citizens and American institutions. The utopia to which human rights activism aspires—an international legal order with the capacity to enforce penalties against states—is inimical to the American conception that rights derive their legitimacy from the exercise of national popular sovereignty. Europeans and Canadians, for example, may feel that American death penalty statutes are a violation of the right to life in Article 3 of the Universal Declaration, but a majority of Americans believe that such statutes are the expression of the democratically expressed will of the people.[20] Hence international human rights objections are seen as both irrelevant and intrusive.[21]

HUMAN RIGHTS AND NATIONALISM

American congressional objections to international human rights instruments may seem to be an expression of American "exceptionalism" or "imperialism," depending on one's point of view. Yet Americans are hardly the only people to believe that their own civil and political rights are both more legitimate and more valuable than the rights enshrined in international covenants. In most liberal democracies, citizens look first to their domestic rights and remedies, and only when these are exhausted or denied do they turn to human rights conventions and international bodies. National groups who do not have states of their own—Kurds, Kosovar Albanians, and Tamils—certainly make use of human rights language to denounce their oppression, but for ultimate remedy they seek statehood for themselves and the right to create a framework of political and legal protection for their people.

International human rights has furthered the growth of nationalism, since human rights covenants have encouraged, if not endorsed the core claim of nationalist movements to collective self-determination. But colonial groups and oppressed minorities have put more faith in obtaining a state of their own than in the protection of international human rights regimes. The classic case of this preference for national rights rather than human rights is, of course, the state of Israel. The Universal Declaration was, in large measure, a response to the torment of the Jewish people. Yet the survivors' overwhelming desire to create a Jewish state, capable of defending Jews everywhere against oppression, reveals that they trusted more to the creation of a state of their own than to the uncertain benefits of universal human rights protection within other people's national states.

Those who stand most in need of human rights protection in the modern world—homeless, stateless peoples, minorities at the mercy of other ethnic or religious majorities—tend to seek collective self-determination, preferably in the form of a defensible state of their own or, if the situation allows, self-rule within an autonomist or federal association with another people. Collective self-government provides defensible rights, legitimized by popular sovereignty and enforced by local courts, police, and punishments. No wonder nationalist movements that promise this solution seem attractive to stateless, homeless, rightless peoples around the world.

Yet nationalism solves the human rights problems of the victorious national groups while producing new victim groups, whose human rights situation is made worse. Nationalists tend to protect the rights of majorities and deny the rights of minorities. Even if one grants that collective self-determination on nationalist lines is going to

be the preference of most persecuted groups seeking
rights protection in the modern world, there still remains
an important place for universalist human rights regimes.
Minorities need the right to appeal against particularist
and unjust rights rulings by the ethnic majorities they live
beside. This is especially the case—as in the example of
Israel—where ethnic majorities rule peoples who are not
citizens and who do not come under full constitutional
protection of national laws. In places like the occupied
territories of the West Bank, Palestinian subjects of Israeli
military rule stand in need of both international and domestic rights monitoring and protection.

Even societies that do fully incorporate minorities into
national rights regimes benefit from the remedies provided by international human rights. All societies need a
juridical source of legitimacy for the right to refuse legal
but immoral orders. Human rights is one such source.
The most essential message of human rights is that there
are no excuses for the inhuman use of human beings. In
particular, there is no valid justification for the abroga-
tion of decency and due process on the grounds of national security, military necessity, or states of siege and
emergency. At most, rights protections can be suspended
in cases of ultimate necessity, but these suspensions of
rights must be justified before legislatures and courts of
law, and they must be temporary.

Another essential function of international human
rights covenants, even in societies with well-ordered national rights regimes, is to provide a universalist vantage
point from which to criticize and revise particularistic national law. The European Convention on human rights
has provided this vantage point for the national rights

b/c Htes are universal

regimes of European states since 1952, and comparison between its standards and those of national states has worked to improve and advance the rights protection afforded by national legislation.

So this is where we are after fifty years of a human rights revolution. Most human beings depend for their rights on the states they live in; those who do not have states of their own aspire to one and in some cases are fighting for one. Yet even though the nation-state remains the chief source of rights protection, international human rights movements and covenants have gained significant influence over national rights regimes. Although the "default settings" of the international order continue to protect state sovereignty, in practice the exercise of state sovereignty is conditional, to some degree, on observance of proper human rights behavior. When states fail in this regard, they render themselves subject to criticism, sanction, and, as a final resort, intervention.

ESTABLISHING THE LIMITS OF HUMAN RIGHTS

As international human rights has gained power and authority, its scope and remit have become increasingly blurred. What precise balance is to be struck between international human rights and state sovereignty? When is intervention justified to reverse human rights abuses in another state? Failure to provide coherent answers to these problems has resulted in increasing uncertainty as to how far the writ of international human rights should run.

The juridical, advocacy, and enforcement revolutions have dramatically raised expectations, and it is unsurprising that the reality of human rights practice should disappoint. The rights and responsibilities implied in the discourse of human rights are universal, yet resources—of time and money—are finite. When moral ends are universal, but means are limited, disappointment is inevitable. Human rights activism would be less insatiable, and less vulnerable to disappointment, if activists could appreciate the degree to which rights language itself imposes— or ought to impose—limits upon itself.

The first limit is a matter of logic and formal consistency. Because the very purpose of rights language is to protect and enhance individual agency, rights advocates must, if they are to avoid contradicting their own principles, respect the autonomy of those agents. Likewise, at the collective level, rights language endorses the desire of human groups to rule themselves. If this is so, human rights discourse must respect the right of those groups to define the type of collective life they wish to lead, provided that this life meets the minimalist standards requisite to the enjoyment of any human rights at all.

Human rights activists accept this limit in theory—but tend to soften it into the vague requirement to display cultural sensitivity in the application of moral universals. In reality, the limit is something more. If human rights principles exist to validate individual agency and collective rights of self-rule, then human rights practice is obliged to seek consent for its norms and to abstain from interference when consent is not freely given. Only in strictly defined cases of necessity—where human life is at risk—can coercive human rights interventions be justified. These norms of informed consent operate inside liberal democratic states to protect human subjects from well-intentioned but potentially harmful medical interventions. The same rules of informed consent need to govern human rights interventions. If, for example, religious groups determine that women should occupy a subordinate place within the rituals of the group, and this place is accepted by the women in question, there is no warrant to intervene on the grounds that human rights considerations of equality have been violated.[22] Human rights principles themselves imply that groups that do not actively persecute others or actively harm their own members should enjoy as much autonomy as the rule of law allows.[23]

Establishing the limits of human rights as a language of moral intervention is all the more important because at least one source of power that held Western human rights in check is now in ruins. There were two human rights cultures after 1945, not just one. The Communist rights tradition—which put primacy on economic and social rights—kept the capitalist rights tradition—emphasizing political and civil rights—from overreaching itself. Since the Helsinki Final Act of 1975, in which the Soviet bloc conceded the right of its citizens to have human rights organizations, there has been one global human rights culture. The collapse of Communism leaves the West freer than before to undertake interventions in the affairs of delinquent or collapsed states. But these interventions have served to blur rather than clarify the proper line between the rights of states and the rights of citizens who may be oppressed within these states. As the West intervenes ever more frequently but ever more inconsistently in the affairs of other societies, the legitimacy of its rights standards is put into question. Human rights is increasingly seen as the language of a moral imperialism just as ruthless and just as self-deceived as the colonial hubris of yesteryear.

Human rights might become less imperial, if it became more political, that is, if it were understood as a language, not for the proclamation and enactment of eternal verities, but as a discourse for the adjudication of conflict. But thinking of human rights in this way means accepting that human rights principles themselves conflict. Activists who suppose that the Universal Declaration of Human Rights is a comprehensive list of all the desirable ends of human life fail to understand that these ends—liberty and equality, freedom and security, private property and distributive justice—conflict, and, because they do, the rights that define them as entitlements are also in conflict. If rights conflict and there is no unarguable order of moral priority in rights claims, we cannot speak of rights as trumps.[24] The idea of rights as trumps implies that when rights are introduced into a political discussion, they serve to resolve the discussion. In fact, the opposite is the case. When political demands are turned into rights claims, there is a real risk that the issue at stake will become irreconcilable, since to call a claim a right is to call it nonnegotiable, at least in popular parlance.[25] Compromise is not facilitated by the use of rights claim language. So if rights are not trumps, and if they create a spirit of nonnegotiable confrontation, what is their use? At best, rights create a common framework, a common set of reference points that can assist parties in conflict to deliberate together. Common language, however, does not necessarily facilitate agreement. In the American abortion debate, for example, both sides agree

[Handwritten marginalia: "Problems w/ rights: only rights can trump other rights language —"]

that the inhuman use of human life should be prohibited, and that human life is entitled to special legal and moral protections.[26] Yet this is hardly common ground at all, since the two sides disagree as to when human life commences, and as to whether the claims of the mother or the unborn child should prevail. This example suggests that it is an illusion to suppose that the function of human rights is to define a higher realm of shared moral values that will assist contending parties to find common ground. Broad evaluative consensus about human rights may be a necessary condition for deliberative agreement, but it is not a sufficient one. Other political factors are essential for closure: shared exhaustion with the conflict, dawning mutual respect, joint mutual recognition—all these must be present, as well as common commitment to moral universals, if agreement is to be reached.

The larger illusion I want to criticize is that human rights is above politics, a set of moral trump cards whose function is to bring political disputes to closure and conclusion. Shared human rights talk can do something to reconcile parties provided that each side listens with respect to the other's particularist inflection of universal claims. Beyond that, rights language raises the stakes. It reminds disputants of the moral nature of their claims. This can be productive. When two sides recognize one another's claim of right, the dispute ceases to be—in their eyes—a conflict between right and wrong and becomes a conflict between competing rights. The resolution of these competing rights claims never occurs in the abstract kingdom of ends, but in the kingdom of means. Human rights is nothing other than a politics, one that must reconcile moral ends to concrete situations and must be prepared to make painful compromises not only between means and ends, but between ends themselves.

But politics is not just about deliberation. Human rights language is also there to remind us that there are some abuses that are genuinely intolerable, and some excuses for these abuses that are insupportable. Rights talk, therefore, helps us to know when deliberation and compromise have become impossible. Hence human rights talk is sometimes used to assemble the reasons and the constituencies necessary for the use of force. Given the conflictual character of rights, and given the fact that many forms of oppression will not answer to argument and deliberation, there are occasions, which must be strictly defined, when human rights as politics becomes a fighting creed, a call to arms.

HUMAN RIGHTS AND SELF-DETERMINATION

From being the insurgent creed of activists during the Cold War, human rights has become "mainstreamed" into the policy framework of states, multilateral lending institutions like the World Bank, and the United Nations itself. The foreign policy rhetoric of most Western liberal states now repeats the mantra that national interests must be balanced by due respect for values, chief of which is human rights. But human rights is not just an additional item in the policy priorities of states. If taken seriously, human rights values put interests into question, interests such as sustaining a large export sector in a nation's defense industry, for example. It becomes incoherent for states like Britain and the United States to condemn Indonesia or Turkey for their human rights performance *values v. Interests*

while providing their military with vehicles or weapons that can be used for the repression of civilian dissent. When values do not actually constrain interests, an "ethical foreign policy"—the self-proclaimed goal of Britain's Labour government—becomes a contradiction in terms.

This is not the only practical problem in reconciling values and interests in dealing with states that violate human rights. There is the additional conflict between furthering the human rights of individuals and maintaining the stability of the nation-state system. Why should stability be of concern to human rights activists? Simply because stable states provide the possibility for national rights regimes, and these remain the most important protector of individual human rights.

States in the age of human rights have to reconcile human rights observance with containing a dissident or oppressed opposition or an ethnic minority seeking self-determination. These secessionist challenges, often backed up by terrorism, sometimes jeopardize the unity of the state. Many states, like the United Kingdom in Northern Ireland, have contained secessionist challenges without major violations of human rights. Others, like Turkey and Serbia, have met secessionist challenges with regimes of repression that sacrifice human rights. Even when secessionist challenges are not explicit, repressive regimes raise the specter of their threat to justify authoritarian rule. China justifies human rights abuses as the price required to maintain the unity of a continental nation-state subject to many regional, ethnic, religious, and tribal pressures. Whenever human rights complaints are aired within earshot of the Chinese leadership, they are quick to invoke the specter of civil war—in other words,

like India - Satanic Verses controversy

to argue that furthering human rights and maintaining state stability are ultimately incompatible.

Much of this is special pleading in defense of the privileges and political monopoly of the party in power. Chinese human rights activists insist that the best long-term guarantee of Chinese national unity is a democratic regime that respects human rights.[27] They also point out that trade liberalization and free markets do not necessarily bring human rights and democracy in their wake. It is quite conceivable to combine authoritarian politics with free markets, despotic rule with private property. When capitalism enters the gates of a closed society, it does not necessarily function as a Trojan horse for human rights. Human rights come to authoritarian societies when activists risk their lives and create a popular and indigenous demand for these rights, and when their activism receives consistent and forthright support from influential nations abroad.

We need not be detained by the special pleading of authoritarian, one-party regimes, but there is much more of a conflict between human rights and state stability when the regime in question is not oppressively authoritarian and when the human rights demands come in the form of a collective demand for territorial autonomy, self-rule, or secession. In these situations, Western states want to promote human rights, but not at the price of dismembering viable democracies and adding to the number of failed, collapsed, or disunited states in the world system. Most states in the post–Cold War era skate around this tension in the fundamental goals of their policy: both supporting human rights and propping up states whose stability is deemed to be essential.

24

Some human rights activists deny this conflict between state stability and human rights. They claim that the best guarantee of state stability has to be democracy, human rights, and fairness in the states in question. In the long run this may be true; but in the short term—where most governments actually live—democracy and human rights often conflict, and popular sovereignty for a majority is often achieved at the cost of ethnic cleansing for a minority. Sometimes the conflicts unleashed by the coming of democracy shatter the state altogether, plunging all human groups into a war of all against all.

The overwhelming problem of the post–Cold War world system has been the fragmentation of state order in three key sectors of the globe—the Balkans, the Great Lakes region of Africa, and the southern Islamic frontier of the former Soviet Union.[28] Obviously these regions have fragmented in part because of the flagrant human rights abuses committed by ethnic majority tyrannies that tried—and failed—to create stable nation-states. But in part fragmentation also results from the destructive impact of demands for territorial autonomy and independence on the part of secessionist groups. Western governments watching the slide of these regions into endemic civil war are justified in concluding that restoring stability—even if it is authoritarian and undemocratic—matters more than either democracy or human rights. Stability, in other words, may count more than justice. Most Western states are finessing this moral triage between rights and stability. They proclaim human rights as their goal, while aiding or investing in states with derisory human rights records. While this is usually seen as a

Is stability > justice?

problem of hypocrisy—not matching words to deeds—in fact it represents a fundamental conflict of principle.

The issues at stake can be illustrated by consideration of the case of the Kurds. They are not campaigning simply to improve their civic position as individuals but to achieve self-determination as a people. Kurdish human rights campaigns are not essentially individual and apolitical in character. They represent a demand for collective self-determination that challenges the governmental authority of Turkey, Syria, Iran, and Iraq. It is by no means obvious how autonomy for the Kurds can be reconciled in practice with the territorial integrity of these states. Because the West fails to face this conflict in its own principles, its interventions satisfy no one. The Turks regard Western human rights criticism as meddling in their internal affairs, while the Kurds regard Western support for their struggle as false and disingenuous.

The Kurdish case also illustrates the political naïveté that so often diminishes the effectiveness of human rights advocacy. For too long human rights has been seen simply as a form of apolitical humanitarian rescue for oppressed individuals. Thus human rights advocates campaign on behalf of groups or individuals imprisoned or oppressed by the states in the region without squarely facing up to the political issue—which is how to find a constitutional framework in the four states that have a Kurdish minority that will guarantee their rights, without creating a dynamic toward independence that would drive the region into civil war. None of the states in question will submit to outside interference. The only viable option is a long and persistent negotiation between Western governments and the nations in the region—a negotiation aimed at relaxing the unitary national ideologies of the countries concerned so that minority groups like the Kurds can find ways to protect their own linguistic and historical heritage with forms of autonomy and constitutionally protected minority rights.[29] Unfortunately, Western states have a stronger interest in conciliating Turkey as a trusted ally in a volatile region than they do in pushing it to change its constitution. A further alibi for Western inaction is violent Kurdish factionalism. It is difficult to represent the interests of a victim community when its elites waste their energies fighting among themselves, yet neither independent human rights organizations nor Western governments have it in their power to put an end to the Kurdish power struggle. Since large-scale constitutional reordering in the Kurdish region is rightly seen as an illegitimate interference in the sovereignty of established states, Western states with human rights agendas are forced back to a strategy of quiet diplomacy that places two-way bets: one on the government in power, another, smaller bet on the oppressed minority. It discreetly aids both, while undermining each, with consequences that actually devalue the legitimacy of its own moral language.

The same inability to reconcile human rights values with maintaining state stability has bedeviled Western policy toward Indonesia. Since 1975 journalists and human rights activists have denounced the Indonesian seizure and occupation of the former Portuguese colony of East Timor. But as long as Indonesia was regarded as a bulwark of the East Asian security system of the United States, as long as the territorial integrity of the huge island archipelago was seen as the overriding objective of

Western policy, nothing was done to stop Indonesian oppression of the East Timorese. How, then, are we to explain why in 1998 the West suddenly began to take a sustained interest in the human rights situation in East
Timor? With the collapse of the Soviet regime, there was
no longer a credible Communist threat in East Asia to
justify further appeasement of the Indonesian military.
Second, the overthrow of Suharto by the students and the
East Asian economic crisis weakened the Indonesian regime so that it could no longer resist human rights pressure. Finally, an indigenous human rights movement,
championed by able and courageous individuals, was
making the Indonesian human rights record a matter of
real embarrassment in the international arena, at a time
when Indonesia needed international credits and diplomatic support. This confluence of pressures led Indonesia to accede to demands for a referendum in East
Timor, which Western observers duly supervised. But the
UN Security Council supposed that it could help the East
Timorese achieve self-determination, while doing nothing to protect them from the wrath of the pro-Indonesian
militias. In effect, the Security Council granted their
claim to self-determination without respecting their need
for security. The consequences were easy to predict: the
massacre of civilians, the economic destruction of an already poor country, and finally the inevitable dispatch of
a peacekeeping force onto what remains the sovereign
territory of Indonesia.

Have we sufficiently attended to the probable consequences of this intervention for the territorial integrity of
Indonesia? If East Timor successfully secedes, how many
other parts of a complex multiethnic, multilingual, multi-

confessional state will also seek independence? It may prove impossible to reconcile self-determination for the East Timorese with the long-term territorial integrity of Indonesia as it now exists. Even accepting that East Timor is a special case—a former colony illegally annexed—we seem not to understand that Western intervention may be contributing to the possible disintegration, at high human cost, of the state of Indonesia. If it is said that its disintegration is inevitable anyway, then it still follows that we need a policy that prevents such disintegration from jeopardizing what we intervened to safeguard in the first place, namely, the human rights of ordinary people. For we can be sure that the Indonesian military will not go without a bloody struggle, and we can be certain that self-determination for some groups will be purchased with the blood of the minorities in their midst.

To repeat, the problem in Western human rights policy is that by promoting ethnic self-determination, we may actually endanger the stability that is a precondition for protecting human rights. Having started the ball rolling in Indonesia, we need to help Indonesians decide where it should stop: whether secessionist claims by other minorities can be contained within a devolved Indonesian democracy, or whether some of these claims will have to result, one day, in statehood.

Beyond the specifics of the Indonesian case, human rights activists need to face up to the fact that human rights advocacy can set in train secessionist pressures that do threaten existing states and may make the human rights situation of ordinary people worse rather than better in the short term. The painful truth is that national self-determination is not always favorable to individual human rights, and democracy and human rights do not necessarily advance hand in hand.

Human Rights, Democracy, and Constitutionalism

In order to reconcile democracy and human rights, Western policy will have to put more emphasis not on democracy alone but on constitutionalism, the entrenchment of a balance of powers, judicial review of executive decisions, and enforceable minority rights guarantees.[3] Democracy without constitutionalism is simply ethnic majority tyranny.

In the face of secessionist claims, which threaten the territorial integrity of nation-states, human rights activists will have to do more than merely champion arrested human rights activists. Nor can they remain neutral in the face of secessionist claims. They will have to develop criteria for understanding which secessionist claims deserve full independence and statehood and which ones can be solved by means of regional autonomy and political devolution. Where groups have sound historical reasons for believing that they cannot live in security and peace alongside another group inside a state, they may have a necessary claim to secession and statehood, based on their right to self-defense. But such claims are not justified everywhere. Where there is no such history of bad blood, no recent history of intercommunal violence, as for example between English Canada and the Québecois, between the English and the Scots, secessionist claims may best be met with devolution and autonomy within the existing nation-state. Devolutionist solutions tend to protect minority rights more effectively than separationist ones. In a territory where an ethnic majority has self-government, it remains bound by the federal constitution signed with the other ethnic majority to respect its own minorities. When outright separation occurs, this pattern of mutual rights supervision no longer takes place within shared institutions.

Where a state is democratic, secessionist demands for self-determination should be contained within the framework of that state wherever possible; but where a state is not democratic, where it opposes all devolution to minorities and denies them protection of their educational, linguistic, and cultural rights, secession and independence become inevitable.[31]

Yet the case of Sri Lanka, where there has been a secessionist movement among the minority Tamil population since 1983 against the Sinhala-dominated government, indicates just how difficult it is to reconcile minority rights, state sovereignty, and individual human rights. After independence from Britain in 1947, there was substantial, and deeply resented, discrimination against the Tamil language together with denial of access to state employment. But violence—in which both sides then took part—did not begin until the 1980s. To reward a secessionist claim with independence now would be to reward a terrorist movement with a great deal of blood on its hands. It would also transfer political control over the Tamil people to the hands of a group with no democratic credentials. In so doing, secession might confer collective self-determination on the Tamils in the form of single-party dictatorship, and this would achieve self-determination for the Tamils as a people, while delivering them up as individuals to tyranny. In these circumstances, the best guarantee of individual Tamil rights and of collective protection of their language and culture would be not the separate statehood demanded by the secessionist movement but substantial self-government and autonomy for the Tamil people within the framework of a democratic Sri Lankan state no longer dominated by the Sinhala majority.[32]

This example should indicate, first, that there are substantial dangers for the human rights of individuals if the international community were to concede statehood to secessionist groups who back their campaign with terror; second, that any resolution of these minority rights claims requires more supple, less unitary and intransigent states. Indeed, the problem is not just getting the state and the insurgent minority to respect human rights. A long-term solution requires an institutional setting in which the state is no longer communalized, no longer seen as the monopoly of any particular confessional, ethnic, or racial group, in which the state is reinvented as the arbiter of a civic pact among ethnic groups. Constitutionalism and the civic state are the institutional sine qua non of effective human rights protection in multiethnic states.

Constitutionalism implies loosening up the unitary nation-state—one people, one nation, one state—so that it can respond adequately to the demands of minorities for protection of their linguistic and cultural heritage, and for their right to self-government. But communalization becomes inevitable in poor countries where the state—with its resources, perquisites, and privileges—remains the major source, not merely of political power, but of social and economic prestige as well. Ethnic conflict is at its most intense in societies, like the former Communist state of Yugoslavia or a desperately poor state like Rwanda, where control of state power is the unique source of all social, political, and economic privilege. Breaking the zero-sum game of ethnic competition for state power requires enlarging social and economic sources of privilege independent of the state, so that even if minority groups can never prevail democratically against majorities, they can secure independent sources of wealth, privilege, and prestige. If so, they do not need to seek secession and can remain within a state democratically dominated by another ethnic group. The South African white minority, for example, has a secure place within the institutions of the economy and society of a black South Africa. Their power in the economy effectively protects them from the adverse effects of majority rule. An independent civil society, therefore, is the essential economic basis for multiethnic pluralism, but also for constitutionalism. Being committed to constitutionalism and human rights, therefore, means a comprehensive strategy of economic and social development as well, aimed at creating an independent and plural civil society. Only then can state institutions sustain the checks and balances that protect minorities against ethnic majority tyranny. Conversely, as in Mugabe's Zimbabwe, where the regime has decided to make war on an independent civil society, in this case, the white farming elite, it must also make war on constitutionalism, on the independence of the judiciary, since this is the main bulwark against the arbitrariness of the regime.

Beyond making the nation-state more flexible toward

minority rights claims, the international order needs to strengthen multinational and regional organizations so that they can grant rights of participation to nations and autonomist regions. This allows nations that do not have states of their own to enter the international arena and advance their interests without having to insist on full sovereignty and further fragment the state system. The European Community allows Catalans, Scots, Basques, and other nonstate peoples to participate in fora promoting the development of their regions. The Organization for Cooperation and Security in Europe (OSCE) helps substate groups and national minorities to find representation and protection in the international arena. The OSCE's minority rights commissioner has done pioneering work with the Baltic states, helping them to revise their citizenship and language laws in order to protect the rights of the Russian minority.[33] In this way, three small states maintain their national independence without creating a casus belli with their former imperial occupier, while minorities inside these states know that powerful European institutions are keeping watch over their interests.[34]

In the transnational legal order now emerging, state sovereignty will become less absolute and national identity less unitary. As a result, human rights within states will be protected by overlapping jurisdictions. Regional rights bodies—like the OSCE—will have more oversight over minority rights problems in member states, and they will do so simply because emerging states conclude that surrendering some of their sovereignty on these issues is worth the price of full admission to the regional club. As sovereignty is more permeable and more controlled, minorities will feel less afraid, and therefore less responsive to secessionist appeals.

Yet it is utopian to look forward to an era beyond state sovereignty. Instead of regarding state sovereignty as an outdated principle, destined to pass away in the era of globalization, we need to appreciate the extent to which state sovereignty is the basis of order in the international system, and that national constitutional regimes represent the best guarantee of human rights. This is an unfamiliar, even controversial principle within a human rights community that for fifty years has looked on the state as the chief danger to the human rights of individuals. And so it proved in the age of totalitarian tyranny. Today, however, the chief threat to human rights comes not from tyranny alone, but from civil war and anarchy. Hence we are rediscovering the necessity of state order as a guarantee of rights. It can be said with certainty that the liberties of citizens are better protected by their own institutions than by the well-meaning interventions of outsiders.

So human rights might best be fortified in today's world not by a weakening of already overburdened states but by their being strengthened wherever possible. State failure cannot be rectified by human rights activism on the part of NGOs. What is required when states fail is altogether more ambitious: regional powers brokering peace accords between factions; peacekeeping forces to ensure that truces stick; multilateral assistance to build national institutions, like tax collection, police forces, courts, and basic welfare services. The aim of the exercise is to create states strong enough and legitimate enough to recover their monopoly over the means of violence, to impose order and create the rule of law. Governments that accord their citizens security without democracy are preferable to no government at all.

It is not merely that democracy may not be possible; there may also be an objection in principle as to our right to insist on it. In *The Law of Peoples*, John Rawls imagines a society called Kazanistan that debars full political participation for those not of Muslim faith but tolerates the religious and private rights of other religious and ethnic minorities. Such a state lives at peace within the international system, even if it does not meet all criteria of human rights equality. It is not obvious that there *is* a Kazanistan, but if there were, there is nothing in Rawls's view—or mine—that would mandate interference in the domestic affairs of such a state. Liberal democrats, Rawls argues, need to accept that state forms other than their own may provide adequate procedural fairness and minority rights protection.[35]

This is not the only lesson that human rights activists from Western liberal democracies may need to learn. The other lesson is that universality properly implies consistency. It is inconsistent to impose international human rights constraints on other states unless we accept the jurisdiction of these instruments on our own. Anglo-Canadians have no business telling Latvia, Lithuania, and Estonia what to do about Russian minority rights unless they accept an obligation to subscribe to OSCE standards in their own treatment of French and aboriginal minorities. Americans have no business lecturing other countries about their human rights performance unless they are prepared to at least enter into dialogue with international rights bodies about sensitive areas—capital punish-

36

[handwritten notes in margin and bottom]
But Singer's argument - is debate over prison conditions as morally important as starving people elsewhere? or people being persecuted for their religious belief?

ment and the conditions in American prisons, for example—that may be in contravention of international rights norms. The obligation to at least engage in dialogue is clear, and the obligation that nations actually practice what they preach is the minimum requirement for a legitimate and effective human rights policy.

Human Rights and Military Intervention

Where all order in a state has disintegrated and its people have been delivered up to a war of all against all, or where a state is engaging in gross, repeated, and systematic violence against its own citizens, the only effective way to protect human rights is direct intervention, ranging from sanctions to the use of military force. Since 1991, this "right of humanitarian intervention" has been asserted by governments seeking to justify interventions in Haiti, Somalia, Iraq, Bosnia, and Kosovo.[36] The armed forces of the Western powers have been busier since 1989 than they ever were during the Cold War, and the legitimizing language for this activity has been the defense of human rights. Yet the juridical status of a right of intervention is exceedingly unclear.[37] While the UN Charter calls on states to proclaim human rights, it also prohibits the use of force against other states and forbids internal interference. The human rights covenants that states have signed since 1945 have implied that state sovereignty is conditional on adequate human rights observance, yet this conditionality has never been made explicit in international law, except in the human rights instruments of the European continent. Elsewhere, the gulf in international law between the nonintervention language of the charter and the interventionist implications of human rights covenants has never been bridged.

Drafters of the Universal Declaration explicitly assumed that the Declaration would warrant interventions where human rights abuse was flagrant. As René Cassin, one of the drafters of the Declaration, put it in 1946, "when repeated or systematic violation of human rights by a given state within its borders results in a threat to international peace (as was the case of the Third Reich after 1933), the Security Council has a right to intervene and a duty to act."[38]

In practice, of course, states have been exceedingly wary of the right of intervention, and when they have intervened, they have done so as a temporary measure. Thus where a state fails in its elementary obligations— maintaining physical security and an adequate food supply for its population—or where its army and police are engaged in sustained violence against minority or dissident political groups, it may temporarily forfeit its rights of sovereign immunity within the international system. But the forfeiture is temporary. Northern Iraq remains under the formal jurisdiction of the government in Baghdad, while in practice Allied aircraft patrolling overhead prevent any effective exercise of Iraqi sovereignty in the Kurdish enclave. Kosovo, for example, is under UN protectorate, but UN Security Council Resolution 1244 explicitly reaffirms that the territory remains under Yugoslav sovereignty.

This idea that interventions do not eradicate or supersede the sovereignty of the defaulting party, merely suspend it, is our attempt to provide universal human rights protection to endangered groups within states without abrogating the sovereignty of that state. We hold onto the importance of state sovereignty for another reason, which is to prevent intervention from becoming imperial. Both our human rights norms and the UN Charter outlaw the use of military power for territorial aggrandizement or occupation. Hence our military interventions are intended to be self-limiting. We are intervening not to take over territory but to bring peace and stability and then get out; our mandate is to restore self-determination, not to extinguish it. Managing these conflicting tensions has not been easy. We are now firmly ensconced in long-term protectorates in Bosnia, Kosovo, and East Timor, behaving like imperial police with imperial obligations and no exit in sight.

Looking at the interventions we have undertaken since the end of the Cold War, who can say that we have been successful? In Bosnia, the intervention has not created a stable self-governing society. Instead we have frozen an ethnic civil war in place. We have not succeeded in anchoring a human rights culture in shared institutions.

Intervention, rather than reinforcing respect for human rights, is consuming their legitimacy, both because our interventions are unsuccessful and because they are inconsistent. And we cannot solve our problem by not intervening at all. In 1994, the UN Security Council stood by and did nothing while hundreds of thousands of Tutsis were massacred by a centrally directed plan of genocide organized by the Hutu-dominated government of Rwanda. Failing to intervene in Rwanda has proved even more damaging to the credibility of human rights principles than late and partial interventions in Iraq, Bosnia, and Kosovo.

So what are we to do? If human rights are universal, human rights abuses everywhere are our business. But we simply cannot intervene everywhere. If we do not ration our resources, how can we possibly be effective? Rationing is both inevitable and necessary, yet there needs to be a clear basis to justify these decisions.

Three criteria have emerged in the late 1990s for the rationing of interventions: (1) the human rights abuses at issue have to be gross, systematic, and pervasive; (2) they have to be a threat to international peace and security in the surrounding region; and (3) military intervention has to stand a real chance of putting a stop to the abuses.

In practice, a fourth criterion comes into play: the region in question must be of vital interest, for cultural, strategic, or geopolitical reasons, to one of the powerful nations in the world and another powerful nation does not oppose the exercise of force. Intervention in Kosovo was justified on this mixture of human rights and national interest grounds: the human rights violations endured by the Kosovars threatened to destabilize Albania, Macedonia, and Montenegro and constituted a threat to the peace and security of the region.

The national interest criterion is supposed to limit the ambit of moral concern, in fact, to trump values. But in Kosovo and Bosnia, values and interests were nearly indistinguishable. The NATO powers intervened to make values prevail, to safeguard the territorial integrity of neighboring states, and, most important of all, to demonstrate the credibility of NATO when faced with a challenge from a defiant leader of a small state.

But values and interests do not always point policy in

the same direction. The idea of national interest implies that where gross human rights abuses do *not* threaten the peace and security of a region, military intervention is not warranted. Burma's repression of civilian dissent may be a clear violation of international human rights norms, but so long as its military rulers do not constitute a threat to their neighbors, they run no risk of military intervention.

There are cases, however, where purely domestic repression rises to such a level that while interests say, "Stay out," values cry, "Go in." The Rwandan genocide ought to have been such a case, but since Western countries could not articulate a pressing national interest for undertaking the risks involved in military action, they stood by and watched 800,000 people die, leaving many Africans to conclude that our supposed commitment to universal values was fatally compromised by racial partiality. In reality, Rwanda was never a purely internal genocide, and our failure to stop it is a direct cause of the widening collapse of state order in the whole of central Africa.

The Rwandan case illustrates that the line between internal and external conflict is hard to draw; that the national interest criterion that keeps us from interfering is not so clear as its defenders claim it to be; and, finally, that atrocities may be so terrible that we are bound to intervene even when they do not impinge on any direct national interest.

Even when a state's domestic behavior is not a clear and present danger to the international system, it is a reliable predictor that it is likely to be so in the future. Consider the example of Hitler's regime, 1933–38, or Stalin's in the same period. In hindsight, there seems no doubt that Western governments' failure to sanction or even condemn their domestic policies encouraged both dictators to believe that their international adventures would go unpunished and unresisted.

So the line between purely domestic human rights abuses and those that threaten international peace and security is unclear, and the deferred or future costs of remaining silent about domestic abuses can be terrible indeed. Yet the rule against intervening in other people's states protects weak states against stronger ones and guarantees a minimum degree of equality among national communities in the world arena. Moreover, the nonintervention rule acts as a restraint on intemperate, premature, and ill-judged forms of coercion. It gives time for sanctions, diplomacy, and negotiation to work. But if they fail, what then? There are no peaceful diplomatic remedies when we are dealing with a Hitler, a Stalin, a Saddam, or a Pol Pot.

If force is an inescapable feature of human rights protection, the question then becomes whether we need to change the default setting of the international system, which is currently set against intervention. Most small states believe that any formalized right of intervention would constitute an encouragement to intervention that would in turn erode the sovereignty of rights-observing and rights-violating states alike. But those in favor believe that the international system needs to formalize in words what it already subscribes to in practice: that state sovereignty is conditional on human rights performance, and that, where this performance threatens international peace and security, the Security Council should have the right to mandate a graduated set of coercive responses ranging from sanctions to full-scale military intervention. The failure to formalize a right of intervention under the UN system simply means that coalitions of the willing who wish to intervene will do so by bypassing the authorizing process of the United Nations altogether.[39]

Changing the default of the international system may or may not be desirable. In practice, there is as little chance of a change in the UN Charter language on intervention as there is of substantive Security Council veto reform or enlargement. We are thus stuck with enforcing human rights in the twenty-first century through an international system drafted by the victors of 1945. As a result, interventions will rarely command international consensus because the institutions do not exist to create such consensus. Human rights may be universal, but support for coercive enforcement of their norms will never be universal. Because interventions will lack full legitimacy, they will have to be limited and partial, and as a result, they will be only partially successful.

MEANS AND ENDS

The legitimacy of human rights standards in the new century will be further compromised by the gulf that has opened up between the universalistic values we proclaim and the risk-averse means we choose to defend them. Since the end of the Cold War, Western nations, acting through the Security Council, have repeatedly promised to protect civilians caught in the middle of civil wars or menaced by rogue regimes. Such promises were made by the UN military mission to Rwanda, by the UN peacekeepers in Srebrenica.[40] In both cases, large populations trusted our moral promises, and their trust was horribly betrayed. I do not need to rehearse the Srebrenica catastrophe here.[41] A comprehensive report to the UN secretary-general has already drawn the necessary lessons: if the United Nations offers to protect civilians in safe havens, its member states must provide heavy armor and air cover and issue robust rules of engagement that allow attacking forces to be engaged and repulsed. This is not a job for lightly armed peacekeepers. Indeed, peacekeeping itself is out of date. It has a limited role in the supervision of truce and border lines established after conflicts between states. Most of the wars since 1989 are internal conflicts between crumbling or disintegrating state armies and a variety of insurgent militias. Both sides use ethnic cleansing as a weapon of war in the drive to create defensible territories with ethnically homogenous populations. In these conditions, there is not only no peace to keep but no credible position of neutrality either. In these situations, human rights protection can be undertaken only as part of peace-enforcement operations in which the international community aligns with the side more nearly in the right and uses military force robustly to stop human rights abuse and create conditions for the reestablishment of stable state order in the region.

Any military or humanitarian intervention amounts to a moral promise to persons in need. If we make promises of this sort, we owe it to ourselves and those we intend to help to devise the military strategy, rules of engagement, and chain of command necessary to make good on our promises. Our failure to do so—in Rwanda and in Bosnia—has undermined the credibility of human rights values in zones of danger around the world. Innocent civilians in danger now have no good reason to trust any promise of protection made by UN peacekeepers. The impact on human rights norms has been catastrophic.

INTERVENTION AS A REWARD FOR VIOLENCE

Intervention is also problematic because we are not necessarily coming to the rescue of pure innocence. Intervention frequently requires us to side with one party in a civil war, and the choice frequently requires us to support parties who are themselves guilty of human rights abuses.

The early warning systems of our democracies sound the alarm only when victims turn to terror and reprisal. For all the earnest talk about the importance of early intervention and prevention, the international community rarely commits resources to a problem before violence has broken out. But this in turn compromises the legitimacy of human rights interventions, for brutal violations of human rights appear to be their prerequisite. The Kosovo Liberation Army committed human rights abuses against Serbian civilians and personnel in order to trigger reprisals, which would in turn force the international community to intervene on their behalf.[42] The KLA's success between 1997 and 1999 was a vintage demonstration of how to exploit the human rights conscience of the West in order to incite an intervention that resulted eventually in guerrilla victory.

For several years, the West hesitated before the choice it had to make. It could either sit by and watch Kosovo descend into full-scale civil war, which threatened to destabilize Albania, Macedonia, or Montenegro, or it could intervene and attempt to control the rollout of Kosovan self-determination. Gradually, it chose the second option. But this military intervention, when it came in March 1999, then unleashed a genuine human rights disaster: the forcible eviction of 800,000 Kosovan citizens to Albania and Macedonia, followed by the massacre of up to 10,000 of those who remained.

The Western allies said they were waging a war for the sake of human rights. In reality, they were dragged into a war by an oppressed ethnic majority whose guerrilla army itself committed human rights abuses. Having been dragged into a war, the West then found itself unable to stop a flood of human rights abuses unleashed as a response to intervention. And even now, the West hesitates over the ultimate question of whether Kosovo should achieve full status as an independent state. Kosovan Albanians who feel that the human rights abuses they have suffered at the hands of the Serbs validate their claim to statehood now feel betrayed by the West; while the West feels equally betrayed by the the wholesale eviction of Serbs that followed the liberation of Kosovo. This enormously complicates the issue of Kosovo's final status, for granting Kosovars full independence appears to reward a secessionist movement that used terror. An indefinite UN protectorate in Kosovo seems the only solution, since it postpones the necessity of deciding Kosovo's final status. Yet an indefinite protectorate amounts to imperialism, and this violates the anti-imperial ethos of our human rights commitment.[43]

Some human rights activists profess to be untroubled by the West's assumption of an unlimited and indefinite "human rights protectorate" in the whole Balkan region.

cosmopolitanism

They believe a profound and long-term shift of the balance of power away from nation-states is underway. For many human rights activists, state sovereignty is an anachronism in a global world. They wish to see ever more global oversight, ever more power to the international human rights community, ever more human rights protectorates. But is this wise? All forms of power are open to abuse, and there is no reason why power that legitimizes itself in the name of human rights should not end up as open to abuse as any other. Those who will end up with more power may only be those who have power already: the coalitions of the willing, the Western nations with the military might necessary for any successful human rights intervention.

rebuttal

The only outcome in Kosovo consistent with our principles is one that moves the province toward effective self-government by its own people and away from administration by UN, NATO, and European Community personnel. Either we believe that people should rule themselves or we do not. A prolonged imperial administration of the south Balkans, justified in the name of human rights, will actually end up violating the very principles it purports to defend.

So, to summarize the political dimensions of the human rights crisis: we are intervening in the name of human rights as never before, but our interventions are sometimes making matters worse. Our interventions, instead of reinforcing human rights, may be consuming their legitimacy as a universalistic basis for foreign policy.

The crisis of human rights relates first of all to our failure to be consistent—to apply human rights criteria to the strong as well as to the weak; second, to our related failure to reconcile individual human rights with our commitment to self-determination and state sovereignty; and third, to our inability, once we intervene on human rights grounds, to successfully create the legitimate institutions that alone are the best guarantee of human rights protection.

These problems of consistency have consequences for the legitimacy of human rights standards themselves. Non-Western cultures look at the partial and inconsistent way we enforce and apply human rights principles and conclude that there is something wrong with the principles themselves. The political failure, in other words, has cultural consequences. It has led the cultures of the non-Western world to view human rights as nothing more than a justification for Western moral imperialism. Failure to be consistent in enforcement and clear about the boundaries of state sovereignty has led to an intellectual and cultural challenge to the universality of the norms themselves. This is the subject of my second essay.

NOTES

1. Primo Levi, *If This Is a Man*, trans. Stuart Woolf (London: Abacus, 1987), pp. 111–12. The significance of the passage was pointed out to me by Alain Finkielkraut's *L'Humanité perdue: essai sur le 20ième siècle* (Paris: Seuil, 1996), pp. 7–11.

2. Richard Rorty, *Truth and Moral Progress: Philosophical Papers* (Cambridge: Cambridge University Press, 1998), p. 11.

3. A. H. Robertson and J. G. Merrills, *Human Rights in the World*, 4th ed. (London: Manchester University Press, 1986), chap. 1; Johannes Morsink, *The Universal Declaration of Human Rights: Origins, Drafting and Intent* (Philadelphia: University of Pennsylvania Press, 1998).

4. Paul Gordon Lauren, *The Evolution of International Human Rights: Visions Seen* (Philadelphia: University of Pennsylvania Press, 1998), p. 269; also Yael Danieli et al., eds., *The Universal Declaration of Human Rights: Fifty Years and Beyond* (New York: Baywood, 1998).

5. Geoffrey Robertson, *Crimes against Humanity: The Struggle for Global Justice* (London: Allen Lane, 1999), pp. 51–54.

6. Luke Clements and James Young, eds., *Human Rights: Changing the Culture* (Oxford: Blackwell, 1999); see also Andrew Moravcsik, "The Origins of Human Rights Regimes: Democratic Delegation in Postwar Europe," *International Organization* 54, no. 2 (Spring 2000): 217–53.

7. United States Department of State, *1999 Country Reports on Human Rights* (Washington, D.C., 1999), introduction.

8. T. F. Homer-Dixon, *Environment, Scarcity, and Violence* (Princeton: Princeton University Press, 1999); O. Mehmet, E. Mendes, and R. Sinding, *Towards a Fair Global Labour Market: Avoiding a New Slave Trade* (London: Routledge, 1999); see also Amnesty International, *Human Rights: Is It Any of Your Business?* (London: Amnesty, 2000); Carnegie Council on Ethics and International Affairs, "Who Can Protect Workers' Rights?" *Human Rights Dialogue* 2, no. 4 (Fall 2000).

9. René Cassin, *La Pensée et l'action* (Paris: Lalou, 1972); John P. Humphrey, *Human Rights and the United Nations: A Great Adventure* (Dobbs Ferry, N.Y.: Transnational, 1984); Eleanor Roosevelt, *On My Own* (London: Hutchinson, 1959), chap. 8; Mary Ann Glendon, *A World Made New: Eleanor Roosevelt and the Universal Declaration of Human Rights* (New York: Random House, 2001).

10. William Korey, *NGO's and the Universal Declaration of Human Rights* (New York: St. Martin's Press, 1998); see also Margaret Keck and Kathryn Sikkink, *Activists beyond Borders: Advocacy Networks in International Politics* (Ithaca: Cornell University Press, 1998).

11. See, for example, Irina Ratushinskaya, *Grey Is the Colour of Hope* (New York: Knopf, 1988).

12. Kenneth Anderson, "After Seattle: NGO's and Democratic Sovereignty in an Era of Globalization" (unpublished essay, Harvard Law School, autumn 2000). I am grateful to Ken Anderson for letting me see this paper.

13. Lauren, *Evolution of International Human Rights*, p. 32; P. M. Kielstra, *The Politics of Slave Trade Suppression in Britain and France, 1814–48* (London: Macmillan, 2000).

14. Korey, *NGO's and the Universal Declaration of Human Rights*, chap. 3.

15. United Nations High Commissioner for Human Rights, Reports and Statements (Geneva, Switzerland, 1999). See also Tom Farer and Felice Gaer, "The UN and Human Rights: At the End of the Beginning," in *United Nations, Divided World: The UN's Role in International Relations*, ed. Adam Roberts and Benedict Kingsbury (Oxford: Clarendon Press, 1993), pp. 240–96.

16. Michael Ignatieff, *Virtual War: Kosovo and Beyond* (London: Chatto and Windus, 2000), pp. 115–37; Sara Sewall and Carl Kaysen, eds., *The United States and the International Criminal Court* (New York: Rowman and Littlefield, 2000).

17. Kenneth Roth, "The Court the US Doesn't Want," *New York Review*, November 19, 1998; see also David Rieff, "Court of Dreams," *New Republic*, September 7, 1998; and Robertson, *Crimes against Humanity*, pp. 300–341.

18. The phrase "rights narcissism" is my own and figures in my "Out of Danger," *Index on Censorship* 3 (1998): 98.

19. Paul Kahn, "Hegemony" (unpublished paper, Yale Law School, January 2000). I am indebted to Paul Kahn for letting me see this essay in advance of publication.

20. David Rieff, "Death Row," *Los Angeles Times Book Review*, February 13, 2000; also H. A. Bedau, ed., *The Death Penalty in America: Current Controversies* (New York: Oxford University Press, 1999); Amnesty International, *The Death Penalty: List of Abolitionist and Retentionist Countries* (London: Amnesty, 1999).

21. Amnesty International, *Rights for All: Country Report, The USA* (London: Amnesty, 1998).

22. Avishai Margalit and Moshe Halbertal, "Liberalism and the Right to Culture," *Social Research* 61, no. 3 (Fall 1994).

23. Will Kymlicka, *Multicultural Citizenship* (Oxford: Clarendon Press, 1995), pp. 107–31.

24. Ronald Dworkin, *Taking Rights Seriously* (Cambridge: Harvard University Press, 1977).

25. Mary Ann Glendon, *Rights Talk: The Impoverishment of Political Discourse* (New York: Free Press, 1991).

26. Ronald Dworkin, *Life's Dominion: An Argument about Abortion, Euthanasia, and Individual Freedom* (New York: Knopf, 1993).

27. Wei Jing Sheng, "The Taste of the Spider," *Index on Censorship* 3 (1998): 30–38; see also U.S. Department of State, *1999 Country Reports on Human Rights: China.*

28. See Mary Kaldor, *New and Old Wars: Organized Violence in a Global Era* (London: Polity, 1999); see also Michael Ignatieff, *Blood and Belonging: Journeys into the New Nationalism* (London: Vintage, 1993).

29. On Kurdistan, see Ignatieff, *Blood and Belonging*, pp. 176–212; P. G. Kreyenbroek and S. Sperl, *The Kurds* (London: Routledge, 1991).

30. Fareed Zakaria, "The Rise of Illiberal Democracy," *Foreign Affairs*, November/December 1997, 22–43; Louis Henkin, *Constitutionalism, Democracy and Foreign Affairs* (New York: Columbia University Press, 1990); see also Anthony Lewis, "Yes to Constitutions and Judges That Enforce Them," *International Herald Tribune*, January 7, 2000.

31. Robert McCorquodale, "Human Rights and Self-Determination," in *The New World Order: Sovereignty, Human Rights and the Self-Determination of Peoples*, ed. Mortimer Sellers (Oxford: Berg, 1996), pp. 9–35; see also Hurst Hannum, *Autonomy, Sovereignty and Self-Determination: The Accommodation of Conflicting Rights* (Philadelphia: University of Pennsylvania Press, 1996).

32. International Center for Ethnic Studies, *Sri Lanka: The Devolution Debate* (Colombo: ICES, 1998); Robert Rotberg, ed., *Creating Peace in Sri Lanka: Civil War and Reconciliation* (Washington, D.C.: Brookings, 1999).

33. Walter Kemp, ed., *Quiet Diplomacy in Action: The OSCE High Commissioner on National Minorities* (Amsterdam: Kluwer, 2000).

34. John Packer, "Problems in Defining Minorities," in *Minority and Group Rights in the New Millennium*, ed. D. Fottreell and B. Bowring (Amsterdam: Kluwer, 1999), pp. 223–74; see also *The Oslo Recommendations regarding the Linguistic Rights of National Minorities* (The Hague: Foundation on Inter-Ethnic Relations, 1998).

35. John Rawls, *The Law of Peoples* (Cambridge: Harvard University Press, 1999), pp. 75–78.

36. Bernard Kouchner, *Le Malheur des autres* (Paris: Grasset, 1993); Kofi Annan, *The Question of Intervention* (New York: United Nations, 1999).

37. Gerry J. Simpson, "The Diffusion of Sovereignty: Self-Determination in the Post-Colonial Age," in Sellers, *The New World Order*, p. 55; Christopher Greenwood, "International Law, Just War and the Conduct of Modern Military Operations," in *Ethical Dilemmas of Military Interventions*, ed. Patrick Mileham and Lee Willet (London: RIIA, 1999), pp. 1–9.

38. M. G. Johnson and Janusz Symonides, *The Universal Declaration of Human Rights: A History of Its Creation and Implementation, 1948–1998* (Paris: UNESCO, 1998), p. 32.

39. Advisory Council on International Affairs, "Humanitarian Intervention" (Amsterdam, 2000; see www.aiv-advice.nl); also Danish Institute of International Affairs, "Humanitarian Intervention: Legal and Political Aspects" (Copenhagen, 1999).

40. On the UN military role in Rwanda, see Romeo Dallaire, "The End of Innocence: Rwanda, 1994," in *Hard Choices: Moral Dilemmas in Humanitarian Intervention*, ed. Jonathan Moore (New York: Rowman and Littlefield, 1998), pp. 71–87.

41. UN Office of the Secretary-General, "Srebrenica Report," pursuant to UNGA Resolution 53/35 (1998), November 15, 1999; see also "Report of the Panel on UN Peace Operations," UN General Assembly, August 21, 2000.

42. See Michael Ignatieff, "The Dream of Albanians," *New Yorker*, January 11, 1999; see also Michael Ignatieff, "Balkan Physics," *New Yorker*, May 10, 1999; and Human Rights Watch, *Human Rights Abuses in Kosovo* (New York: Human Rights Watch, 1993); *Humanitarian Law Violations in Kosovo* (New York: Human Rights Watch, 1998); *A Week of Terror in Drenica: Humanitarian Law Violations in Kosovo* (New York: Human Rights Watch, 1999).

43. Independent International Commission on Kosovo, *The Kosovo Report* (New York: Oxford University Press, 2000).

Human Rights as Idolatry

FIFTY YEARS after its proclamation, the Universal Declaration of Human Rights has become the sacred text of what Elie Wiesel has called a "world-wide secular religion."[1] UN Secretary-General Kofi Annan has called the Declaration the "yardstick by which we measure human progress." Nobel Laureate Nadine Gordimer has described it as "the essential document, the touchstone, the creed of humanity that surely sums up all other creeds directing human behavior."[2] Human rights has become the major article of faith of a secular culture that fears it believes in nothing else. It has become the lingua franca of global moral thought, as English has become the lingua franca of the global economy.

The question I want to ask about this rhetoric is this: if human rights is a set of beliefs, what does it mean to believe in it? Is it a belief like a faith? Is it a belief like a hope? Or is it something else entirely?

Human rights is misunderstood, I shall argue, if it is seen as a "secular religion." It is not a creed; it is not a metaphysics. To make it so is to turn it into a species of idolatry: humanism worshiping itself. Elevating the moral and metaphysical claims made on behalf of human rights may be intended to increase its universal appeal. In fact, it has the opposite effect, raising doubts among religious and non-Western groups who do not happen to be in need of Western secular creeds.

It may be tempting to relate the idea of human rights to propositions like the following: that human beings have an innate or natural dignity, that they have a natural and intrinsic self-worth, that they are sacred. The problem with these propositions is that they are not clear and they are controversial. They are not clear because they confuse what we wish men and women to be with what we empirically know them to be. On occasion, men and women behave with inspiring dignity. But that is not the same thing as saying that all human beings have an innate dignity or even a capacity to display it. Because these ideas about dignity, worth, and human sacredness appear to confuse what is with what ought to be, they are controversial, and because they are controversial, they are likely to fragment commitment to the practical responsibilities entailed by human rights instead of strengthening them. Moreover, they are controversial because each version of them must make metaphysical claims about human nature that are intrinsically contestable. Some people will have no difficulty thinking human beings are sacred, because they happen to believe in the existence of a God who created Mankind in His likeness. People who do not believe in God must either reject that human beings are sacred or believe they are sacred on the basis of a secular use of religious metaphor that a religious person will find unconvincing. Foundational claims of this sort divide, and these divisions cannot be resolved in the way humans usually resolve their arguments, by means of discussion and compromise. Far better, I would argue, to forgo these kinds of foundational arguments altogether and seek to build support for human rights on the basis of what such rights actually *do* for human beings.

People may not agree why we have rights, but they can agree that we need them. While the foundations for human rights belief may be contestable, the prudential grounds for believing in human rights protection are much more secure. Such grounding as modern human rights requires, I would argue, is based on what history tells us: that human beings are at risk of their lives if they lack a basic measure of free agency; that agency itself requires protection through internationally agreed standards; that these standards should entitle individuals to oppose and resist unjust laws and orders within their own states; and, finally, that when all other remedies have been exhausted, these individuals have the right to appeal to other peoples, nations, and international organizations for assistance in defending their rights. These facts may have been demonstrated most clearly in the catastrophic history of Europe in the twentieth century, but there is no reason in principle why non-European peoples cannot draw the same conclusions from them, or why in ages to come the memory of the Holocaust and other such crimes will not move future generations to support the universal application of human rights norms.

A prudential—and historical—justification for human rights need not make appeal to any particular idea of human nature. Nor should it seek its ultimate validation in a particular idea of the human good. Human rights is an account of what is right, not an account of what is good. People may enjoy full human rights protection and still believe that they lack essential features of a good life. If this is so, shared belief in human rights ought to be compatible with diverging attitudes concerning what constitutes a good life. In other words, a universal regime of human rights protection ought to be compatible with moral pluralism. That is, it should be possible to maintain regimes of human rights protection in a wide variety of civilizations, cultures, and religions, each of which happens to disagree with others as to what a good human life should be. Another way of putting the same thought is that people from different cultures may continue to disagree about what is good, but nevertheless agree about what is insufferably, unarguably wrong. The universal commitments implied by human rights can be compatible with a wide variety of ways of living only if the universalism implied is self-consciously minimalist. Human rights can command universal assent only as a decidedly "thin" theory of what is right, a definition of the minimum conditions for any kind of life at all.

Even then it may not be minimal enough to command universal assent. An appropriately political sense of human rights must accept that it is a fighting creed and that its universal claims will be resisted. No authority whose power is directly challenged by human rights advocacy is likely to concede its legitimacy. The bias of human rights advocacy must be toward the victim, and the test of legitimacy—and hence of universality—is what might be termed the victim's consent. If victims do freely seek human rights protection, rights language applies. The objections of those who engage in oppression can be heard—as to facts about whether oppression is or is not occurring— but the claims of victims should count more than the claims of oppressors. Still, victims cannot enjoy unlimited rights in the definition of what constitutes an abuse. A human rights abuse is something more than an inconvenience, and seeking human rights redress is distinct from seeking recognition. It is about protecting an essential exercise of human agency. Hence while it is the victim's claim of abuse that sets a human rights process moving, a victim remains under an obligation to prove that such an abuse genuinely occurred.

Human rights matter because they help people to help themselves. They protect their agency. By agency, I mean more or less what Isaiah Berlin meant by "negative liberty," the capacity of each individual to achieve rational intentions without let or hindrance. By rational, I do not necessarily mean sensible or estimable, merely those intentions that do not involve obvious harm to other human beings. Human rights is a language of individual empowerment, and empowerment for individuals is desirable because when individuals have agency, they can protect themselves against injustice. Equally, when individuals have agency, they can define for themselves what they wish to live and die for. In this sense, to emphasize agency is to empower individuals, but also to impose limits on human rights claims themselves. To protect human agency necessarily requires us to protect all individuals' right to choose the life they see fit to lead. The usual criticism of this sort of individualism is that it imposes a Western conception of the individual on other cultures. My claim is the reverse: that moral individualism protects cultural diversity, for an individualist position must respect the diverse ways individuals choose to live their lives. In this way of thinking, human rights is only a systematic agenda of "negative liberty," a tool kit against oppression, a tool kit that individual agents must be free to use as they see fit within the broader frame of cultural and religious beliefs that they live by.

Why should this "minimalist" justification for human rights be necessary? Why should it matter that we find a way to reconcile human rights universalism with cultural and moral pluralism? Since 1945 human rights language has become a source of power and authority. Inevitably, power invites challenge. Human rights doctrine is now so powerful, but also so unthinkingly imperialist in its claim to universality, that it has exposed itself to serious intellectual attack. These challenges have raised important questions about whether human rights deserves the authority it has acquired; whether its claims to universality are justified, or whether it is just another cunning exercise in Western moral imperialism.

There are three distinct sources of the cultural challenge to the universality of human rights. Two come from outside the West: one from resurgent Islam, the second from East Asia; and the third, from within the West itself. Each of these is independent of the others; but taken together, they have raised substantial questions about the cross-cultural validity and hence legitimacy of human rights norms.

THE ISLAMIC CHALLENGE

The challenge from Islam has been there from the beginning.[3] When the Universal Declaration was being drafted in 1947, the Saudi Arabian delegation raised particular objection to Article 16, relating to free marriage choice, and Article 18, relating to freedom of religion. On the question of marriage, the Saudi delegate to the committee examining the draft of the Universal Declaration made an argument that has resonated ever since through Islamic encounters with Western human rights:

> The authors of the draft declaration had, for the most part, taken into consideration only the standards recognized by western civilization and had ignored more ancient civilizations which were past the experimental stage, and the institutions of which, for example, marriage, had proved their wisdom through the centuries. It was not for the Committee to proclaim the superiority of one civilization over all other[s] or to establish uniform standards for all countries of the world.[4]

This was simultaneously a defense of the Islamic faith and a defense of patriarchal authority. The Saudi delegate in effect argued that the exchange and control of women is the very raison d'être of traditional cultures, and that the restriction of female choice in marriage is central to the maintenance of patriarchal property relations. On the basis of these objections to Articles 16 and 18, the Saudi delegation refused to ratify the Declaration.

There have been recurrent attempts, including Islamic Declarations of Human Rights, to reconcile Islamic and Western traditions by putting more emphasis on family duty and religious devotion, and by drawing on distinctively Islamic traditions of religious and ethnic toleration.[5] But these attempts at syncretic fusion between Islam and the West have never been entirely successful: agreement by the parties actually trades away what is vital to each side. The resulting consensus is bland and unconvincing.

Since the 1970s the Islamic reaction to human rights has grown more hostile. Ever since the Islamic Revolution in Iran rose up against the tyrannical modernization of the shah, Islamic figures have questioned the universal writ of Western human rights norms. They have pointed out that the Western separation of church and state, secular and religious authority, is alien to the jurisprudence and political thought of the Islamic tradition. The freedoms articulated in the Universal Declaration make no sense within the theocratic bias of Islamic political thought. The right to marry and found a family, to freely choose one's partner, is a direct challenge to the authorities in Islamic society that enforce the family choice of spouse, polygamy, and the keeping of women in purdah. In Islamic eyes, universalizing rights discourse implies a sovereign and discrete individual, which is blasphemous from the perspective of the Holy Koran.

In responding to this challenge, the West has made the mistake of assuming that fundamentalism and Islam are synonymous. Islam speaks in many voices, some more anti-Western, some more theocratic than others. National contexts may be more important in defining local Islamic reactions to Western values than broad theological principles in the religion as a whole. Where Islamic societies have managed to modernize, create a middle class, and enter the global economy—Egypt and Tunisia being examples—a constituency in favor of basic human rights can emerge. Egypt, for instance, is in the process of passing legislation to give women the right to divorce; and although dialogue with Egypt's religious authorities has been difficult, women's rights will be substantially enhanced by the new legislation.[6] In Algeria, a secular human rights culture is more embattled. A secularizing elite who rode to power after a bloody anticolonial revolution failed to modernize their country. It now faces an opposition, led by Islamic militants, which has taken an anti-Western, anti–human rights direction. And in Afghanistan, where the state itself has collapsed and foreign arms transfers have aggravated the nation's decline, the Taliban movement has arisen, explicitly rejecting all Western human rights standards. In these instances, the critical variant is not Islam itself—a protean, many-featured religion—but the fateful course of Western policy and economic globalization itself.

But there is another Western reaction to the Islamic challenge that is equally ill-conceived. There is a style of cultural relativism that concedes too much to the Islamic challenge. For the last twenty years, an influential current in Western political opinion has been maintaining, in the words of Adamantia Pollis and Peter Schwab, that human rights is a "Western construct of limited applicability," a twentieth-century fiction, dependent on the rights traditions of America, Britain, and France and therefore inapplicable in cultures that do not share this historical matrix of liberal individualism.[7]

This current of thought has complicated intellectual origins: the Marxist critique of the rights of man, the anthropological critique of the arrogance of late-nineteenth-century bourgeois imperialism, and the postmodernist critique of the universalizing pretensions of European Enlightenment thought.[8] All of these tendencies have come together in a critique of Western intellectual hegemony as expressed in the language of human rights. Human rights is seen as an exercise in the ning of Western reason: no longer able to dominate the world through direct imperial rule, Western reason masks its own will to power in the impartial, universalizing language of human rights and seeks to impose its own narrow agenda on a plethora of world cultures that do not actually share the West's conception of individuality, selfhood, agency, or freedom. This postmodernist relativism began as an intellectual fashion on Western campuses, but it has seeped slowly into Western human rights practice, causing all activists to pause and consider the intellectual warrant for the universality they once took for granted.

ASIAN VALUES

This challenge within has been amplified by a challenge from without: the critique of Western human rights standards by some political leaders in the rising economies of East Asia. While the Islamic challenge to human rights can be explained in part by the failure of Islamic societies to benefit from the global economy, the Asian challenge is a consequence of the region's staggering economic success. Because of Malaysia's robust growth rate, its leaders, for example, feel confident enough to reject Western ideas of democracy and individual rights in favor of an Asian route to development and prosperity—which depends on authoritarian government and authoritarian family structures. The same can be said about Singapore, which combined political authoritarianism with market capitalism in a successful synthesis. Singapore's Lee Kuan Yew has been quoted as saying that Asians have "little doubt that a society with communitarian values where the interests of society take precedence over that of the individual suits them better than the individualism of America." This Singaporean model cites rising divorce and crime rates in the West in order to argue that Western individualism is subversive of the order necessary for the enjoyment of rights themselves.[9] An "Asian model" puts community and family ahead of individual rights and order ahead of democracy and individual freedom. In reality, of course, there is no single Asian model: each of these societies has modernized in different ways, within different political traditions, and with differing degrees of political and market freedom. Yet it has proven useful for Asian authoritarians to argue that they represent a civilizational challenge to the hegemony of Western models.[10]

Let it be conceded at once that these three separate challenges to the universality of human rights discourse—two from without, one from within the Western tradition—have had a productive impact. They have forced human rights activists to question their assumptions, to rethink the history of their commitments, and to realize just how complicated intercultural dialogue on rights questions becomes when all cultures participate as equals.

HUMAN RIGHTS AND INDIVIDUALISM

Having said this, however, I would argue that Western defenders of human rights have traded too much away. In the desire to find common ground with Islamic and Asian positions and to purge their own discourse of the imperial legacies uncovered by the postmodernist critique, Western defenders of human rights norms compromising the very universality they ought to be defending. They also risk rewriting their own history.

Many traditions, not just Western ones, were represented at the drafting of the Universal Declaration of Human Rights—the Chinese, Middle Eastern Christian, but also Marxist, Hindu, Latin American, Islamic—and the drafting committee members explicitly construed their task not as a simple ratification of Western convictions but as an attempt to define a limited range of moral universals from within their very different religious, political, ethnic, and philosophic backgrounds.[11] This helps to explain why the document makes no reference to God in its preamble. The Communist delegations would have vetoed any such reference, and the competing religious traditions could not have agreed on the wording of the terms that would make human rights derive from our common existence as God's creatures. Hence the secular ground of the document is not a sign of European cultural domination so much as a pragmatic common denominator designed to make agreement possible across a range of divergent cultural and political viewpoints.

It remains true, of course, that Western inspirations—and Western lawyers—played the predominant role in the drafting of the document. Even so, the drafters' mood in 1947 was anything but triumphalist. They were aware, first of all, that the age of colonial emancipation was at hand: Indian independence was proclaimed while the language of the Declaration was being finalized. Although the Declaration does not specifically endorse self-determination, its drafters clearly foresaw the coming tide of struggles for national independence. Because it does proclaim the right of people to self-government and freedom of speech and religion, it also concedes the right of colonial peoples to construe moral universals in a language rooted in their own traditions. Whatever failings the drafters of the Declaration may be accused of, unexamined Western triumphalism is not one of them. Key drafters like René Cassin of France and John Humphrey of Canada knew the knell had sounded on two centuries of Western colonialism.[12]

They also knew that the Declaration was not so much a proclamation of the superiority of European civilization as an attempt to salvage the remains of its Enlightenment heritage from the barbarism of a world war just concluded. The Universal Declaration is written in full awareness of Auschwitz and dawning awareness of Kolyma. A consciousness of European barbarism is built into the very language of the Declaration's preamble: "whereas disregard and contempt for human rights have resulted in barbarous acts which have outraged the conscience of mankind. . . ."

The Declaration may still be a child of the Enlightenment, but it was written when faith in the Enlightenment faced its deepest crisis of confidence. In this sense, human rights is not so much the declaration of the superiority of European civilization as a warning by Europeans that the rest of the world should not seek to reproduce its mistakes. The chief of these was the idolatry of the nation-state, causing individuals to forget the higher law commanding them to disobey unjust orders. The abandonment of this moral heritage of natural law, the surrender of individualism to collectivism, the drafters believed, led to the catastrophe of Nazi and Stalinist oppression. Unless the disastrous heritage of European collectivism is kept in mind, as the framing experience in the drafting of the Universal Declaration, its individualism will appear to be nothing more than the ratification of Western bourgeois capitalist prejudice. In fact, it was much more: a studied attempt to reinvent the European natural law tradition in order to safeguard individual agency against the totalitarian state.

It remains true, therefore, that the core of the Universal Declaration is the moral individualism for which it is so much reproached by non-Western societies. It is this individualism for which Western activists have become most apologetic, believing that it should be tempered by greater emphasis on social duties and responsibilities to the community. Human rights, it is argued, can recover universal appeal only if it softens its individualistic bias and puts greater emphasis on the communitarian parts of the Universal Declaration, especially Article 29, which says that "everyone has duties to the community in which alone the free and full development of his personality is possible." This desire to water down the individualism of rights discourse is driven by a desire both to make human rights more palatable to less individualistic cultures in the non-Western world and also to respond to disquiet among Western communitarians at the supposedly corrosive impact of individualistic values on Western social cohesion.[13]

But this tack mistakes what rights actually are and misunderstands why they have proven attractive to millions of people raised in non-Western traditions. Rights are meaningful only if they confer entitlements and immunities on individuals; they are worth having only if they can be enforced against institutions like the family, the state, and the church. This remains true even when the rights in question are collective or group rights. Some of these rights—like the right to speak your own language or practice your own religion—are essential preconditions for the exercise of individual rights. The right to speak a language of your choice will not mean very much if the language has died out. For this reason, group rights are needed to protect individual rights. But the ultimate purpose and justification of group rights is not the protection of the group as such but the protection of the individuals who compose it. Group rights to language, for example, must not be used to prevent an individual from learning a language besides the language of the group. Group rights to practice religion should not cancel the right of individuals to leave a religious community if they choose.[14]

Rights are inescapably political because they tacitly imply a conflict between a rights holder and a rights "withholder," some authority against which the rights holder can make justified claims. To confuse rights with aspirations, and rights conventions with syncretic syntheses of world values, is to wish away the conflicts that define the very content of rights. There will always be conflicts between individuals and groups, and rights exist to protect individuals. Rights language cannot be parsed or translated into a nonindividualistic, communitarian framework. It presumes moral individualism and is nonsensical outside that assumption.

Moreover, it is precisely this individualism that renders it attractive to non-Western peoples and explains why human rights has become a global movement. Human rights is the only universally available moral vernacular that validates the claims of women and children against the oppression they experience in patriarchal and tribal societies; it is the only vernacular that enables dependent persons to perceive themselves as moral agents and to act against practices—arranged marriages, purdah, civic disenfranchisement, genital mutilation, domestic slavery, and so on—that are ratified by the weight and authority of their cultures. These agents seek out human rights protection precisely because it legitimizes their protests against oppression.

If this is so, then we need to rethink what it means when we say that rights are universal. Rights doctrines arouse powerful opposition because they challenge powerful religions, family structures, authoritarian states, and tribes. It would be a hopeless task to attempt to persuade these holders of power of the universal validity of rights doctrines, since if these doctrines prevailed, they would necessarily abridge and constrain their exercise of authority. Thus universality cannot imply universal assent, since in a world of unequal power, the only propositions that the powerful and powerless would agree on would be entirely toothless and anodyne ones. Rights are universal because they define the universal interests of the powerless, namely, that power be exercised over them in ways that respect their autonomy as agents. In this sense, human rights is a revolutionary creed, since it makes a radical demand of all human groups, that they serve the interests of the individuals who compose them. This, then, implies that human groups should be, insofar as possible, consensual, or at least that they should respect an individual's right to exit when the constraints of the group become unbearable.

The idea that groups should respect an individual's right of exit is not easy to reconcile with what groups actually are. Most human groups—the family, for example—are blood groups, based on inherited kinship or ethnic ties. People do not choose to be born into them and do not leave them easily, since these collectivities provide the frame of meaning within which individual life makes sense. This is as true in modern secular societies as it is in religious or traditional societies. Group rights doctrines exist to safeguard the collective rights—for example, to language—that make individual agency meaningful and valuable. But individual and group interests inevitably conflict. Human rights exist to adjudicate these conflicts, to define the irreducible minimum beyond which group and collective claims must not go in constraining the lives of individuals.

Even so, adopting the values of individual agency does not necessarily entail adopting Western ways of life. Believing in your right not to be tortured or abused need not mean adopting Western dress, speaking Western languages, or approving of the Western way of life. To seek human rights protection is not to change your civilization; it is merely to avail yourself of the protections of "negative liberty."

Human rights does not—should not—delegitimize traditional culture as a whole. The women in Kabul who come to Western human rights agencies seeking their protection from the Taliban militias do not want to cease being Muslim wives and mothers; they want to combine respect for their traditions with an education and professional health care provided by a woman. They hope the agencies will defend them against being beaten and persecuted for claiming such rights.[15]

The legitimacy of these claims is reinforced by the fact that the people who are making them are not foreign human rights activists but the victims themselves. In Pakistan, it is local human rights groups, not international agencies, that are leading the fight to defend poor country women from "honor killings," being burned alive when they disobey their husbands; it is local Islamic women who are criticizing the grotesque distortion of Islamic teaching that provides justification for such abuse.[16] Human rights has gone global by going local, empowering the powerless, giving voice to the voiceless.

It is simply not the case, as Islamic and Asian critics contend, that human rights forces the Western way of life upon their societies. For all its individualism, human rights does not require adherents to jettison their other cultural attachments. As Jack Donnelly argues, human rights "assumes that people probably are best suited, and in any case are entitled, to choose the good life for themselves."[17] What the Declaration does mandate is the right to choose, and specifically the right to *leave* when choice is denied. The global diffusion of rights language would never have occurred had these not been authentically attractive propositions to millions of people, especially women, in theocratic, traditional, or patriarchal societies.

Critics of this view of human rights diffusion would argue that it is too "voluntaristic": it implies that individuals in traditional societies are free to choose the manner of their insertion into the global economy; free to choose which Western values to adopt and which to reject. In reality, these critics argue, people are not free to choose. Economic globalization steamrolls over local economies, and moral globalization—human rights—follows behind as the legitimizing ideology of global capitalism. "Given the class interest of the internationalist class carrying out this agenda," Kenneth Anderson writes, "the claim to universalism is a sham. Universalism is mere globalism and a globalism, moreover, whose key terms are established by capital."[18] This idea that human rights is the moral arm of global capitalism ignores the insurgent nature of the relation between human rights activism and the global corporation.[19] The NGO activists who devote their lives to challenging the labor practices of global giants like Nike and Shell would be astonished to discover that their human rights agenda has been serving the interests of global capital all along. Anderson conflates globalism and internationalism and mixes up two classes, the free market globalists and the human rights internationalists, whose interests and values are in conflict.

While free markets do encourage the emergence of assertively self-interested individuals, these individuals seek human rights in order to *protect* them from the indignities and indecencies of the market. Moreover, the dignity such individuals are seeking to protect is not necessarily derived from Western models. Anderson writes as if human rights is always imposed from the top down by an international elite bent on "saving the world." He ignores the extent to which the demand for human rights is issuing from the bottom up.

The test of human rights legitimacy, therefore, is take-up from the bottom, from the powerless. Instead of apologizing for the individualism of Western human rights standards, activists need to attend to another problem, which is how to create conditions in which individuals on the bottom are free to avail themselves of such rights as they want. Increasing the freedom of people to exercise their rights depends on close cultural understanding of the frameworks that often constrain choice. The much debated issue of genital mutilation illustrates this point. What may appear as mutilation in Western eyes is simply the price of tribal and family belonging to women; if they fail to submit to the ritual, they no longer have a place within their world. Choosing to exercise their rights, therefore, may result in a social ostracism that leaves them no option but to leave their tribe and make for the city. Human rights advocates have to be aware of what it really means for a woman to abandon traditional practices. But, equally, activists have a duty to inform women of the medical costs and consequences of these practices and to seek, as a first step, to make them less dangerous for women who wish to undergo them. Finally, it is for women themselves to decide how to make the adjudication between tribal and Western wisdom. The criteria of informed consent that regulate medical patients' choices in Western societies are equally applicable in non-Western settings, and human rights activists are under an obligation, inherent in human rights discourse itself, to respect the autonomy and dignity of agents. An activist's proper role is not to make the choices for the women in question but to enlarge their sense of what the choices entail. In traditional societies, harmful practices can be abandoned only when the whole community decides to do so. Otherwise, individuals who decide on their own face ostracism and worse. Consent in these cases means collective or group consent.

Sensitivity to the real constraints that limit individual freedom in different cultures is not the same thing as deferring to these cultures. It does not mean abandoning universality. It simply means facing up to a demanding intercultural dialogue in which all parties come to the table under common expectations of being treated as moral equals. Traditional society is oppressive to individuals within it, not because it fails to afford them a Western way of life, but because it does not accord them a right to speak and be heard. Western activists have no right to overturn traditional cultural practice, provided that such practice continues to receive the assent of its members. Human rights is universal not as a vernacular of cultural prescription but as a language of moral empowerment. Its role is not in defining the content of culture but in trying to enfranchise all agents so that they can freely shape that content.

Empowerment and freedom are not value-neutral terms: they have an unquestionably individualistic bias, and traditional and authoritarian societies will resist these values because they aim a dart at the very habits of obedience that keep patriarchy and authoritarianism in place. But how people use their freedom is up to them, and there is no reason to suppose that if they adopt the Western value of freedom, they will give it Western content. Furthermore, it is up to victims, not outside observers, to define for themselves whether their freedom is in jeopardy. It is entirely possible that people whom Western observers might suppose are in oppressed or subordinate positions will seek to maintain the traditions and patterns of authority that keep them in this subjection. Women are placed in such subordinate positions in many of the world's religions, including ultra-Orthodox Judaism and certain forms of Islam. Some women will come to resent these positions, others will not, and those who do not cannot be supposed to be trapped inside some form of false consciousness that it is the business of human rights activism to unlock. Indeed, adherents may believe that participation in their religious tradition enables them to enjoy forms of belonging that are more valuable to them than the negative freedom of private agency. What may be an abuse of human rights to a human rights activist may not be seen as such by those whom human rights activists construe to be victims. This is why consent ought to be the defining constraint of human rights interventions in all areas where human life itself or gross and irreparable physical harm is not at stake. Where life itself is at stake, those in jeopardy are unlikely to refuse to be saved.

Human rights discourse ought to suppose that there are many differing visions of a good human life, that the West's is only one of them, and that, provided agents have a degree of freedom in the choice of that life, they should be left to give it the content that accords with their history and traditions.

To sum up at this point, Western human rights activists have surrendered too much to the cultural relativist challenge. Relativism is the invariable alibi of tyranny. There is no reason to apologize for the moral individualism at the heart of human rights discourse: it is precisely this that makes it attractive to dependent groups suffering exploitation or oppression. There is no reason, either, to think of freedom as a uniquely Western value or to believe that advocating it unjustly imposes Western values on them. For it contradicts the meaning of freedom itself to attempt to define for others the use they make of it.

The best way to face the cultural challenge to human rights—coming from Asia, Islam, and Western postmodernism—is to admit its truth: rights discourse *is* individualistic. But that is precisely why it has proven an effective remedy against tyranny, and why it has proven attractive to people from very differing cultures. The other advantage of liberal individualism is that it is a distinctly "thin" theory of the human good: it defines and proscribes the "negative," that is, those restraints and injustices that make any human life, however conceived, impossible; at the same time, it does not prescribe the "positive" range of good lives that human beings can lead.[20] Human rights is morally universal because it says that all human beings need certain specific freedoms "from"; it does not go on to define what their freedom "to" should consist in. In this sense, it is a less prescriptive universalism than the world's religions: it articulates standards of human decency without violating rights of cultural autonomy.

Certainly, as Will Kymlicka and many others have pointed out, there are some conditions of life—the right to speak a language, for example—that cannot be protected by individual rights alone. A linguistic minority needs to have the right to educate its children in the language in order for the linguistic community to survive, and it can do this only if the larger community recognizes its collective right to do so. At the same time, however, all collective rights provisions have to be balanced with individual rights guarantees, so that individuals do not end up being denied substantive freedoms for the sake of the group. This is not an easy matter, as any English-speaking Montrealer with experience of Quebec language legislation will tell you. But it can be done, provided individual rights have an ultimate priority over collective ones, so that individuals are not forced to educate their children in a manner that is not freely chosen.[21] Even granting, therefore, that groups need collective rights in order to protect shared inheritances, these rights themselves risk becoming a source of collective tyranny unless individuals retain a right of appeal. It is the individualism of human rights that makes it a valuable bulwark against even the well-intentioned tyranny of linguistic or national groups.

The conflict over the universality of human rights norms is a political struggle. It pits traditional, religious, and authoritarian sources of power against human rights advocates, many of them indigenous to the culture itself, who challenge these sources of power in the name of those who find themselves excluded and oppressed. Those who seek human rights protection are not traitors to their culture, and they do not necessarily approve of other Western values. What they seek is protection of their rights as individuals within their own culture. Authoritarian resistance to their demands invariably takes the form of a defense of the culture as a whole against intrusive forms of Western cultural imperialism. In reality this relativist case is actually a defense of political or patriarchal power. Human rights intervention is warranted not because traditional, patriarchal, or religious authority is primitive, backward, or uncivilized by *our* standards, but by the standards of whose whom it oppresses. The warrant for intervention derives from *their* demands, not from ours.

THE SPIRITUAL CRISIS

Whereas the cultural crisis of human rights has been about the intercultural validity of human rights norms, the spiritual crisis concerns the ultimate metaphysical grounds for these norms. Why do human beings have rights in the first place? What is it about the human species and the human individual that entitles them to rights? If there is something special about the human person, why is this inviolability so often honored in the breach rather than in the observance? If human beings are special, why do we treat each other so badly?

Human rights has become a secular article of faith. Yet the faith's metaphysical underpinnings are anything but clear. Article 1 of the Universal Declaration cuts short all justification and simply asserts: "All human beings are born free and equal in dignity and rights. They are endowed with reason and conscience and should act towards one another in a spirit of brotherhood." The Universal Declaration enunciates rights; it does not explain why people have them.

The drafting history of the Declaration makes clear that this silence was deliberate. When Eleanor Roosevelt first convened a drafting committee in her Washington Square apartment in February 1947, a Chinese Confucian and a Lebanese Thomist got into a stubborn argument about the philosophical and metaphysical bases of rights.

Mrs. Roosevelt concluded that the only way forward lay in West and East agreeing to disagree.[22]

There is thus a deliberate silence at the heart of human rights culture. Instead of a substantive set of justifications explaining why human rights are universal, instead of reasons that go back to first principles—as in Thomas Jefferson's unforgettable preamble to the American Declaration of Independence—the Universal Declaration of Human Rights simply takes the existence of rights for granted and proceeds to their elaboration.

Pragmatic silence on ultimate questions has made it easier for a global human rights culture to emerge. As the philosopher Charles Taylor puts it, the concept of human rights "could travel better if separated from some of its underlying justifications."[23] The Declaration's vaunted "universality" is as much a testament to what the drafters kept *out* of it as to what they put *in.*

The Declaration envisioned a world where, if human beings found their civil and political rights as citizens were taken away, they could still appeal for protection on the basis of their rights as human beings. Beneath the civil and political, in other words, stood the natural. But what exactly is the relationship between human rights and natural rights, or between the human and the natural? What is naturally human?

Human rights is supposed to formalize in juridical terms the natural duties of human conscience in cases where civil and political obligations either prove insufficient to prevent abuses or have disintegrated altogether. Human rights doctrines appear to assume that if the punishments and incentives of governed societies are taken away, human rights norms will remind people of the requirements of natural decency. But this assumes that the capacity to behave decently is a natural attribute. Where is the empirical evidence that this is the case? A more likely assumption is that human morality in general and human rights in particular represent a systematic attempt to correct and counteract the natural tendencies we discovered in ourselves as human beings. The specific tendency we are seeking to counteract is that while we may be naturally disposed, by genetics and history, to care for those close to us—our children, our family, our immediate relations, and possibly those who share our ethnic or religious origins—we may be naturally indifferent to all others outside this circle. Historically, human rights doctrines emerged to counteract this tendency toward particularist and exclusivist ethical circles of concern and care. As Avishai Margalit has put it, "we need morality to overcome our natural indifference for others."[24]

The history immediately antecedent to the Universal Declaration of Human Rights provides abundant evidence of the natural indifference of human beings. The Holocaust showed up the terrible insufficiency of all the supposedly natural human attributes of pity and care in situations where these duties were no longer enforced by law. Hannah Arendt argued in *The Origins of Totalitarianism* that when Jewish citizens of European states were deprived of their civil and political rights, when, finally, they had been stripped naked and could appeal to their captors only as plain, bare human beings, they found that even their nakedness did not awaken the pity of their tormentors. As Arendt put it, "it seems that a man who is nothing but a man has lost the very qualities which make it possible for other people to treat him as a fellow man."[25]

The Universal Declaration set out to reestablish the idea of human rights at the precise historical moment in which they had been shown to have had no foundation whatever in natural human attributes.

All that one can say about this paradox is that it defines the divided consciousness with which we have lived with the idea of human rights ever since. We defend human rights as moral universals in full awareness that they must counteract rather than reflect natural human propensities.

So we cannot build a foundation for human rights on natural human pity or solidarity. For the idea that these propensities are natural implies that they are innate and universally distributed among individuals. The reality—as the Holocaust and countless other examples of atrocity make clear—is otherwise. We must work out a belief in human rights on the basis of human beings as they are, working on assumptions about the worst we can do, instead of hopeful expectations of the best. In other words, we do not build foundations on human nature but on human history, on what we know is likely to happen when human beings do not have the protection of rights. We build on the testimony of fear, rather than on the expectations of hope. This, it seems to me, is how human rights consciousness has been built since the Holocaust. Human rights is one of the achievements of what Judith Shklar once called "the liberalism of fear."[26] Likewise, in 1959, Isaiah Berlin argued that in the post-Holocaust era awareness of the necessity of a moral law is sustained no longer by belief in reason but by the memory of horror. "Because these rules of natural law were flouted, we have been forced to become conscious of them."[27] And what, in his view, were these rules?

> We know of no court, no authority, which could, by means of some recognized process, allow men to bear false witness, or torture freely or slaughter fellow men for pleasure; we cannot conceive of getting these universal principles or rules repealed or altered.

The Holocaust laid bare what the world looked like when pure tyranny was given free rein to exploit natural human cruelty. Without the Holocaust, then, no Declaration. Because of the Holocaust, no unconditional faith in the Declaration either. The Holocaust demonstrates both the prudential necessity of human rights and their ultimate fragility.

If one end product of Western rationalism is the exterminatory nihilism of the Nazis, then any ethics that takes only reason for its guide is bound to seem powerless when human reason begins to rationalize its own exterminatory projects. If reason rationalized the Holocaust, so the argument goes, then only an ethics deriving its ultimate authority from a higher source than reason can prevent a Holocaust in the future. So the Holocaust accuses not just Western nihilism but Western humanism itself and puts human rights in the dock. For human rights is a secular humanism: an ethics ungrounded in divine or ultimate sanction and based only in human prudence.

It is unsurprising, therefore, that in the wake of the Holocaust human rights should face an enduring intellectual challenge from a range of religious sources, Catholic, Protestant, and Jewish, all of whom make the same essential point: that if the purpose of human rights is to restrain the human use of power, then the only authority capable of doing so must lie beyond humanity itself, in some religious source of authority.

Michael Perry, a legal philosopher at Wake Forest University, argues, for example, that the idea of human rights is "ineliminably religious."[28] Unless you think, he says, that human beings are sacred, there seems no persuasive reason to believe that their dignity should be protected with rights. Only a religious conception of human beings as the handiwork of God can sustain a notion that individuals should have inviolable natural rights. Max Stackhouse, a Princeton theologian, argues that the idea of human rights has to be grounded in the idea of God, or at least in the idea of "transcendent moral laws." Human rights needs a theology in order to explain, in the first place, why human beings have "the right to have rights."[29]

From a religious point of view, secular humanism may indeed be putting human beings on a pedestal when they should be down in the mud where they belong. If human rights exists to define and uphold limits to the abuse of human beings, then its underlying philosophy had better define humanity as a beast in need of restraint. Instead, human rights makes humanity the measure of all things, and from a religious point of view this is a form of idolatry. Humanist idolatry is dangerous for three evident reasons: first, because it puts the demands, needs, and rights of the human species above any other and therefore risks legitimizing an entirely instrumental relation to other species; second, because it authorizes the same instrumental and exploitative relationship to nature and the environment; and finally, because it lacks the metaphysical claims necessary to limit the human use of human life, in such instances as abortion or medical experimentation.[30]

What *is* so sacred about human beings? Why, exactly, do we think that ordinary human beings, in all their radical heterogeneity of race, creed, education, and attainment, can be viewed as possessing the same equal and inalienable rights? If idolatry consists in elevating any purely human principle into an unquestioned absolute, surely human rights looks like an idolatry.[31] To be sure, humanists do not literally worship human rights, but we use the language to say that there is something inviolate about the dignity of each human being. This is a worshipful attitude. What is implied in the metaphor of worship is a cultlike credulity, an inability to subject humanist premises to the same critical inquiry to which humanist rationalism subjects religious belief. The core of the charge is that humanism is simply inconsistent. It criticizes all forms of worship, except its own.

To this humanists must reply, if they wish to be consistent, that there *is* nothing sacred about human beings, nothing entitled to worship or ultimate respect. All that can be said about human rights is that they are necessary to protect individuals from violence and abuse, and if it is asked why, the only possible answer is historical. Human rights is the language through which individuals have created a defense of their autonomy against the oppression of religion, state, family, and group. Conceivably, other languages for the defense of human beings could be invented, but this one is what is historically available to human beings here and now. Moreover, a humanist is required to add, human rights language is *not* an ultimate trump card in moral argument. No human language can have such powers. Indeed, rights conflicts and their adjudication involve intensely difficult trade-offs and compromises. This is precisely why rights are not sacred, nor are those who hold them. To be a rights-bearer is not to hold some sacred inviolability but to commit oneself to live in a community where rights conflicts are adjudicated through persuasion, rather than violence. With the idea of rights goes a commitment to respect the reasoned commitments of others and to submit disputes to adjudication. The fundamental moral commitment entailed by rights is not to respect, and certainly not to worship. It is to deliberation.[32] The minimum condition for deliberating with another human being is not necessarily respect, merely negative toleration, a willingness to remain in the same room, listening to claims one doesn't like to hear, for the purpose of finding compromises that will keep conflicting claims from ending in irreparable harm to either side. That is what a shared commitment to human rights entails.

This reply is not likely to satisfy a religious person. From a religious perspective, to believe, as humanists do, that nothing is sacred—although what others hold to be sacred is entitled to protection—is to remove any restraining limits to the exercise of human power.

The idea of the sacred—the idea that there is some realm that is beyond human knowing or representation, some Mount Sinai forever withheld from human sight—is supposed to impose a limit on the human will to power. Even as metaphor—divorced from any metaphysical claim—the sacred connotes the idea that there must be a moral line that no human being can cross. The ideology of human rights is clearly an attempt to define that line. But, from a religious point of view, any attempt to create any strictly secular limit to the exercise of human power is bound to be self-defeating. Without the idea of the nonhuman divine, without the idea of the sacred and the idea of impassable limits, both to reason and to power, there can be no viable protection of our species from ourselves. The dispute comes down to this: the religious side believes that only if humans get down on their knees can they save themselves from their own destructiveness; a humanist believes that they will do so only if they stand up on their own two feet.

This is an old dispute, and each side can marshal powerful historical arguments. The strongest aspect of the religious case is the empirical evidence that men and women, moved by religious conviction, have been able to stand up against tyranny when those without such convictions did not. In the Soviet labor camps, religious people, from convictions as various as Judaism and Seventh Day Adventism, gave inspiring examples of indestructible dignity. Similarly, it was religious conviction that inspired some Catholic priests and laypersons to hide Jews in wartime Poland. Finally, the black movement for civil rights in the United States is incomprehensible unless we remember the role of religious leadership, metaphors, and language in inspiring individuals to risk their lives for the right to vote. These examples carry more weight than metaphysical argument. But secularism has its heroes too. The lyric poet Anna Akhmatova's writing gave voice to the torments of all the women like herself who lost their husbands and children in the Gulag. Primo Levi, a secular Jew and a scientist, gave witness on behalf of those who perished at Auschwitz. His work is exemplary testimony to the capacity of secular reason to describe the enormity of evil. Moral courage draws its resources where it can, and both secular and religious sources have inspired heroes.

If we turn from the sources of heroism to the sources of villainy, the religious cannot claim that the fear of God has prevented humans from doing their worst. The idea that a sense of the sacred is necessary to keep humans moral stands on weak empirical grounds, to say the least. Indeed, sacred purposes have often been pressed into the service of iniquity. Religion, after all, is a foundational doctrine, making claims that it regards as incontestable. The belief that you possess unassailable grounds of faith and that God commands you to spread the faith have provided powerful justifications for torture, forced conversion, the condemnation of heresy, and the burning of heretics. Foundational beliefs of all kinds have been a long-standing menace to the human rights of ordinary individuals.

On the other hand, it is hard to deny the force of the religious counterargument—that the abominations of the twentieth century were an expression of secular hubris, of human power intoxicated by the technology at its disposal and unrestrained by any sense of ethical limit. To the extent that history is a relevant witness, its testimony corroborates neither the believer nor the unbeliever. Before radical evil, both secular humanism and ancient belief have been either utterly helpless victims or enthusiastic accomplices.

So how are we to conclude? A humanist will point out that religions make anthropomorphic claims about the identity of their God while simultaneously claiming that He cannot be represented. This contradiction is idolatrous, but it may be a necessary idolatry; believers must worship something. Their devotions must fall upon some image or object that can give a focus to their prayers. Hence the unavoidable necessity of graven images or representations of divinity in most of the world religions. Idolatry may therefore be a necessary component of any belief. If this is true of religion, it may also be true of humanism. We may not be entitled to worship our species, but our commitment to protect it needs sustaining by some *faith* in our species. Such faith, needless to say, can only be conditional, reasserted in the face of the evidence that we are, upon occasion, worse than swine.

The idea of idolatry calls all believers, secular or religious, to sobriety; it asks them to subject their own enthusiasm, their overflowing sense of righteousness, to a continual scrutiny. Religious persons aware of the dangers of idolatry scrutinize their worship for signs of pride, zeal, or intolerance toward other believers; nonbelievers ought to guard against Voltairian contempt for the religious convictions of others. Such contempt presumes that human reason is capable of assessing the truth content of a competing form of belief. Secular reason has no such power. For both a religious and a secular person, therefore, the metaphor of idolatry acts as a restraint against both credulity and contempt. For secular unbelievers radically misread the story of Exodus if they think it is a warning merely against religious credulity. Surely it is the great mythic warning against human fallibility, both secular and religious, our weakness for idols of our own making, our inability to cease worshiping the purely human. A humanism that worships the human, that takes pride in being human, is surely as flawed as those religious beliefs that purport to *know* God's plans for humans. A humanism that is not idolatrous is a humanism that refuses to make metaphysical claims that it cannot justify, a humanism with the wisdom to respect the dire warnings of Exodus.

Yet even a humble humanism should have the courage to ask why human rights needs the idea of the sacred at all. If the idea of the sacred means that human life ought to be cherished and protected, why does such an idea need theological foundations? Why do we need an idea of God in order to believe that human beings are not free to do what they wish with other human beings; that human beings should not be beaten, tortured, coerced, indoctrinated, or in any way sacrificed against their will? These intuitions derive simply from our own experience of pain and our capacity to imagine the pain of others. Believing that humans are sacred does not necessarily strengthen these injunctions. The reverse is often true: acts of torture or persecution are frequently justified in terms of some sacred purpose. Indeed, the strength of a purely secular ethics is its insistence that there are no "sacred" purposes that can ever justify the inhuman use of human beings. An antifoundational humanism may seem insecure, but it does have the advantage that it cannot justify inhumanity on foundational grounds.

A secular defense of human rights depends on the idea of moral reciprocity: that we judge human actions by the simple test of whether we would wish to be on the receiving end. And since we cannot conceive of any circumstances in which we or anyone we know would wish to be abused in mind or body, we have good reasons to believe that such practices should be outlawed. That we are capable of this thought experiment—that is, that we possess the faculty of imagining the pain and degradation done to other human beings as if it were our own—is simply a fact about us as a species. Because we are all capable of this form of limited empathy, we all possess a conscience, and because we do, we wish to be free to make up our own minds and express those justifications. The fact that there are many humans who remain indifferent to the pain of others does not prove that they do not possess a conscience, merely that this conscience is free. This freedom is regrettable: it makes human beings capable of freely chosen acts of evil, but this freedom is constitutive of what a conscience is. Such facts about human beings— that they feel pain, that they can recognize the pain of others, and that they are free to do good and abstain from evil—provide the basis by which we believe that all human beings should be protected from cruelty. Such a minimalist conception of shared human capacities—empathy, conscience, and free will—essentially describes what is required for an individual to be an agent of any kind. Protecting such an agent from cruelty means empowerment with a core of civil and political rights. Those who insist that civil and political rights need supplementing with social and economic ones make a claim that is true—that individual rights can be exercised effectively only within a framework of collective rights provision— but they may be obscuring the priority relation between the individual and the collective. Individual rights without collective rights may be difficult to exercise, but collective rights without individual ones end up in tyranny.

Moreover, rights inflation—the tendency to define anything desirable as a right—ends up eroding the legitimacy of a defensible core of rights. That defensible core ought to be those that are strictly necessary to the enjoyment of any life whatever. The claim here would be that civil and political freedoms are the necessary condition for the eventual attainment of social and economic security. Without the freedom to articulate and express political opinions, without freedom of speech and assembly, together with freedom of property, agents cannot organize themselves to struggle for social and economic security.

As Amartya Sen argues, the right to freedom of speech is not, as the Marxist tradition maintained, a lapidary bourgeois luxury, but the precondition for having any other rights at all. "No substantial famine has ever occurred," Sen observes, "in any country with a democratic form of government and a relatively free press." The Great Leap Forward in China, in which between twenty-three and thirty million people perished as a result of irrational government policies implacably pursued in the face of their obvious failure, would never have been allowed to take place in a country with the self-correcting mechanisms of a free press and political opposition.[33] So much for the argument so often heard in Asia that a people's "right to development," to economic progress, should come before their right to free speech and democratic government. Such civil and political rights are both an essential motor of economic development in themselves and also a critical guarantee against coercive gov-

ernment schemes and projects. Freedom, to adapt the title of Sen's latest book, *is* development.[34]

Such a secular defense of human rights will necessarily
leave religious thinkers unsatisfied. For them secular humanism is the contingent product of late European civilization and is unlikely to command assent in non-European and nonsecular cultures. Accordingly, a lot of effort
has been expended in proving that the moral foundations of the Universal Declaration are derived from the
tenets of all the world's major religions. The Universal
Declaration is then reinterpreted as the summation of
the accumulating moral wisdom of the ages. Paul Gordon
Lauren begins his history of the idea of human rights
with an inventory of the world's religions, concluding
with the claim that "the moral worth of each person is a
belief that no single civilization or people or nation or
geographical area or even century can claim uniquely as
its own."[35]

This religious syncretism is innocuous as inspirational
rhetoric. But as Lauren himself concedes, only Western
culture turned widely shared propositions about human
dignity and equality into a working doctrine of rights.
This doctrine originated not in Djeddah or Beijing but in
Amsterdam, Siena, and London, wherever Europeans
sought to defend the liberties and privileges of their cities
and estates against the nobility and the emerging national state.

To point out the European origins of rights is not to
endorse Western cultural imperialism. Historical priority
does not confer moral superiority. As Jack Donnelly
points out, the Declaration's historical function was not
to universalize European values but actually to put cer-

tain of them—racism, sexism, and anti-Semitism, for example—under eternal ban.[36] Non-Western foes of human rights take its proclamations of "universality" as an example of Western arrogance and insensitivity. But universality properly means consistency: the West is obliged to practice what it preaches. This puts the West, no less than the rest of the world, on permanent trial.

THE WEST AGAINST ITSELF

In the moral dispute between the "West" and the "Rest," both sides make the mistake of assuming that the other speaks with one voice. When the non-Western world looks at human rights, it assumes—rightly—that the discourse originates in a matrix of historical traditions shared by all the major Western countries. But these Western nations interpret the core principles of their own rights tradition very differently. A common tradition does not necessarily result in common points of view on rights matters. All of the formative rights cultures of the West—the English, the French, and the American—give a different account of such issues as privacy, free speech, incitement, the right to bear arms, and the right to life. In the fifty years since the promulgation of the Universal Declaration, these disagreements within the competing Western rights traditions have become more salient. Indeed, the moral unanimity of the West—always a myth more persuasive from the outside than from the inside—is breaking up and revealing its unalterable heterogeneity. American rights discourse once belonged to the common European natural law tradition and to the British common law. But this sense of a common anchorage now competes with a growing awareness of American moral and legal exceptionalism.

American human rights policy in the last twenty years is increasingly distinctive and paradoxical: it is the product of a nation with a great national rights tradition that leads the world in denouncing the human rights violations of others but refuses to ratify key international rights conventions itself. The most important resistance to the domestic application of international rights norms comes not from rogue states outside the Western tradition or from Islam and Asian societies. It comes, in fact, from within the heart of the Western rights tradition itself, from a nation that, in linking rights to popular sovereignty, opposes international human rights oversight as an infringement on its democracy. Of all the ironies in the history of human rights since the Declaration, the one that would most astonish Eleanor Roosevelt is the degree to which her own country is now the odd one out.

In the next fifty years, we can expect to see the moral consensus that sustained the Universal Declaration in 1948 splintering still further. For all the rhetoric about common values, the distance between America and Europe on rights questions—like abortion and capital punishment—may grow, just as the distance between the West and the Rest may also increase. There is no reason to believe that economic globalization entails moral globalization. Indeed, there is some reason to think that as economies have unified their business practices, ownership, languages, and networks of communication, a countermovement has developed to safeguard the integrity of national communities, national cultures, religions, and indigenous and religious ways of life.

This is a prophecy not of the end of the human rights movement but of its belated coming of age, its recognition that we live in a plural world of cultures that have a right to equal consideration in the argument about what we can and cannot, should and should not, do to human beings. Indeed, this may be the central historical importance of human rights in the history of human progress: it has abolished the hierarchy of civilizations and cultures. As late as 1945, it was normative to think of European civilization as inherently superior to the civilizations it ruled. Many Europeans continue to believe this, but they know that they have no right to do so. More to the point, many non-Western peoples also took the civilizational superiority of their rulers for granted. They no longer have any reason to continue believing this. One reason why this is so is the global diffusion of human rights. It is the language that most consistently articulates the moral equality of all the individuals on the face of the earth. But to the degree that it does, it simultaneously increases the level of conflict over the meaning, application, and legitimacy of rights claims. Rights language says: all human beings belong at the table, in the essential conversation about how we should treat each other. But once this universal right to speak and be heard is granted, there is bound to be tumult. There is bound to be discord. Why? Because the European voices that once took it upon themselves to silence the babble with a peremptory ruling no longer take it as their privilege to do so, and those who sit with them at the table no longer grant them the right to do so. All this counts as progress, as a step toward a world imagined for millennia in different cultures and religions: a world of genuine moral equality among human beings. But if so, a world of moral equality is a world of conflict, deliberation, argument, and contention.

To repeat a point made earlier: We need to stop thinking of human rights as trumps and begin thinking of them as a language that creates the basis for deliberation. In this argument, the ground we share may actually be quite limited: not much more than the basic intuition that what is pain and humiliation for you is bound to be pain and humiliation for me. But this is already something. In such a future, shared among equals, rights are not the universal credo of a global society, not a secular religion, but something much more limited and yet just as valuable: the shared vocabulary from which our arguments can begin, and the bare human minimum from which differing ideas of human flourishing can take root.

NOTES

1. Elie Wiesel, "A Tribute to Human Rights," in *The Universal Declaration of Human Rights: Fifty Years and Beyond,* ed. Y. Danieli et al. (Amityville, N.Y.: Baywood, 1999), p. 3.

2. Nadine Gordimer, "Reflections by Nobel Laureates," in Danieli et al., *Universal Declaration of Human Rights,* p. vii.

3. Katerina Dalacoura, *Islam, Liberalism and Human Rights* (London: I. B. Tauris, 1998); F. Halliday, "The Politics of Islamic Fundamentalism," in *Islam, Globalization and Post-Modernity,* ed. A. S. Ahmed and H. Donnan (London: I. B. Tauris, 1994); A. A. An-Na'im, ed., *Human Rights in Cross-Cultural Perspectives* (Philadelphia: University of Pennsylvania Press, 1992), chap. 1; see also Mehdi Amin Razavi and David Ambuel, eds., *Philosophy, Religion and the Question of Tolerance* (New York: SUNY Press, 1997), chap. 4.

4. Glen Johnson and Janusz Symonides, *The Universal Declaration of Human Rights: A History of Its Creation and Implementation, 1948–1998* (Paris: UNESCO, 1998), pp. 52–53.

5. Paul Gordon Lauren, *The Evolution of International Human Rights: Visions Seen* (Philadelphia: University of Pennsylvania Press, 1998), p. 8.

6. *New York Times,* March 3, 2000.

7. A. Pollis and P. Schwab, eds., *Human Rights: Cultural and Ideological Perspectives* (New York: Praeger, 1979), pp. 1, 4; see also Amitai Etzioni, "Cross-Cultural Judgments: The Next Steps," *Journal of Social Philosophy* 28, no. 3 (Winter 1997).

8. For a Marxist critique of human rights as bourgeois ideology, see Tony Evans, ed., *Human Rights Fifty Years On: A Reappraisal* (Manchester: Manchester University Press, 1998).

9. For a mordant critique of the Singaporean argument, see Ian Buruma, "The King of Singapore," *New York Review,* June 10, 1999. Lee Kuan Yew quoted in the *International Herald Tribune,* November 9–10, 1991.

10. W. T. De Bary, *Asian Values and Human Rights: A Confucian Communitarian Perspective* (Cambridge: Harvard University Press, 1998), pp. 1–16.

11. Johannes Morsink, *The Universal Declaration of Human Rights: Origins, Drafting and Intent* (Philadelphia: University of Pennsylvania Press, 1999).

12. René Cassin, "Historique de la déclaration universelle en 1938," in *La Pensée et l'action* (Paris: Editions Lalou, 1972), pp. 103–18; J. P. Humphrey, *Human Rights and the United Nations: A Great Adventure* (Dobbs Ferry, N.Y.: Transnational, 1984), pp. 46–47.

13. Michael Sandel, *Democracy's Discontents* (Cambridge: Harvard University Press, 1996).

14. Michael Ignatieff, *The Rights Revolution* (Toronto: Anansi, 2000), chap. 3; Will Kymlicka, *Multicultural Citizenship* (Oxford: Clarendon Press, 1995).

15. See Michael Ignatieff, *The Warrior's Honour: Ethnic War and the Modern Conscience* (London: Vintage, 1995), pp. 55–69.

16. See *Murder in Purdah,* BBC Television Correspondent Spe-

cial, January 23, 1999, directed by Giselle Portenier, produced by Fiona Murch.

17. Jack Donnelly, "Human Rights and Asian Values: A Defense of Western Universalism," in *The East Asian Challenge for Human Rights*, ed. Joanne R. Bauer and Daniel A. Bell (Cambridge: Cambridge University Press, 1999), p. 86.

18. Kenneth Anderson, "Secular Eschatologies and Class Interests," in *Religion and Human Rights: Conflicting Claims*, ed. Carrie Gustafson and Peter Juviler (Armonk, N.Y.: M. E. Sharpe, 1999), p. 115.

19. Richard Falk, "The Quest for Human Rights," in *Predatory Globalization: A Critique* (London: Polity, 1999), chap. 6.

20. These distinctions—negative liberty, positive liberty, freedom from, freedom to—are suggested by Isaiah Berlin, "Two Concepts of Liberty," in *The Proper Study of Mankind*, ed. Henry Hardy (London: Chatto and Windus, 1997), pp. 191–243; on "thin" theories of the good, see John Rawls, *A Theory of Justice* (Cambridge: Harvard University Press, 1970).

21. Kymlicka, *Multicultural Citizenship*, pp. 2–6.

22. See Morsink, *The Universal Declaration of Human Rights*.

23. Charles Taylor, "Conditions of an Unforced Consensus on Human Rights," in Bauer and Bell, *The East Asian Challenge for Human Rights*, p. 126.

24. Avishai Margalit, "The Ethics of Memory" (The Horkheimer Lectures, May 1999, Goethe University, Frankfurt). I am grateful to Avishai Margalit for letting me see these lectures in manuscript.

25. Hannah Arendt, *The Origins of Totalitarianism* (New York: Harcourt and Brace, 1973), p. 300.

26. Judith N. Shklar, "The Liberalism of Fear," in *Political Thought and Political Thinkers*, ed. Stanley Hoffman (Chicago: University of Chicago Press, 1998), pp. 3–21.

27. Isaiah Berlin, "European Unity and Its Vicissitudes," in *The Crooked Timber of Humanity* (London: Chatto and Windus, 1991), pp. 204–5.

28. Michael J. Perry, *The Idea of Human Rights: Four Inquiries* (New York: Oxford University Press, 1998), pp. 11–41.

29. Max Stackhouse, "Human Rights and Public Theology," in Gustafson and Juviler, *Religion and Human Rights*, pp. 13, 16.

30. Peter Singer, *Animal Liberation* (New York: Random House, 1990); J. M. Coetzee, *The Lives of Animals* (Princeton: Princeton University Press, 1999).

31. Moshe Halbertal and Avishai Margalit, *Idolatry* (Cambridge: Harvard University Press, 1992).

32. Amy Gutmann and Dennis Thompson, *Democracy and Disagreement* (Cambridge: Harvard University Press, Belknap Press, 1996).

33. Amartya Sen, "Human Rights and Economic Achievements," in Bauer and Bell, *The East Asian Challenge for Human Rights*, pp. 92–93.

34. Amartya Sen, *Development as Freedom* (New York: Oxford University Press, 1999).

35. Lauren, *Evolution of International Human Rights*, p. 11.

36. Donnelly in Bauer and Bell, *The East Asian Challenge for Human Rights*, p. 68.

COMMENTS

Grounding Human Rights

K. ANTHONY APPIAH

THE FIRST part of Michael Ignatieff's characteristically thoughtful and elegant essay draws our attention to three major facts:

First, that there really has been a human rights revolution. In the years since the Universal Declaration of Human Rights of 1948, and with increasing urgency since the end of the Cold War, a great international system of what he calls "juridical, advocacy, and enforcement" instruments has developed for protecting our human rights. These rights are encoded not only in the UN treaties, declarations, and conventions but also in regional agreements, and in much recent constitution making around the world. That is, they have been imported into the legal systems of many states.

A second fact is that it can be hard, in practice, to decide how—or even whether—to exercise the powers of one country or of the community of nations against a single state that fails to observe the norms encoded in those instruments, in the face of the need for stability and order. The demand for respect for individual human rights occurs within the framework of the sovereignty of states, and often a state that abuses human rights remains a better option for its citizens and for the rest of us than anarchy or collapse into long-term civil war.

His third observation is that there is, as a result, a need for serious thought about when, how, and whether the international community should engage in military intervention in defense of the rights of certain citizens when they are abused by the states in which they live.

Let me call these the *three key facts.*

I agree with much of what he says on these topics. Even when I do not, his positions strike me as reasonable, as helpful starting points for a conversation about the issues he raises. But my job here—perhaps the job of philosophy always—is to insist on distinctions and on details, in short, to kibitz, while simultaneously attending to the big picture. I should like, therefore, to make a few methodological observations about the issues he raises in the earlier parts of his essay, to defend a particular view of how we should proceed in thinking about rights, and then to show—this will be the kibitzing—that this requires me to demur about some of the details. I should say at the start that I do not have any wisdom on the question of what the rules of humanitarian intervention should be: this, I agree, is a crucial question, and much of what Michael says about it, I repeat, strikes me as eminently sensible. Let me remind you, however, of his conclusion in this area, because I would like to record here one demurral that is not philosophical but political.

Michael Ignatieff says that

[t]he crisis of human rights relates first of all to our failure to be consistent—to apply human rights criteria to the strong as well as to the weak; second, to our related failure to reconcile individual human rights with our commitment to self-determination

and state sovereignty; and third, to our inability, once we intervene on human rights grounds, to successfully create the legitimate institutions that alone are the best guarantee of human rights protection.

I think, however—here is my demurral—that it is not, as he suggests, necessarily a problem that we recognize the distinction between strong and weak states when we decide what pressures to exercise. For, as he says elsewhere, one fundamental guide in intervention, as in just wars generally, is whether we have the resources to succeed: and success means leaving things better at the end than they were at the start. This makes a difference not only in thinking about military intervention but in other cases: in China, the concern with "face" means that public challenges tend to be less productive than private ones, as Mary Robinson has found as the UN High Commissioner for Human Rights; in Turkey, on the other hand, as earlier in South Africa, being held publicly to certain standards that are thought of as the standards of civilized nations can be effective because it matters (or mattered) to those states that they should be perceived in those ways. Now I very much agree with Michael about one of the cases that he clearly has in mind here: the treatment of prisoners, especially in state as opposed to federal prisons, in the United States, in my view, clearly falls below certain standards to which we are committed by international treaty (and, as it happens, I think, by the American Constitution, properly understood). We—especially we citizens of this country—ought to be insistent that something be done about this if we are sincere in our attachment to those standards. But the fact that the standards are universal and that, therefore, they apply equally everywhere does not mean that we can ignore the distinction between weak and strong states in deciding how to go about trying to get them enforced.

Let me also say at the start that I agree very much with the last of the points in the passage I have just quoted. Systems of law that recognize human rights ought to be instituted and implemented in practice everywhere, and that should be our common aim.

Much of what I will have to say has to do with the second set of questions raised in that summary paragraph: questions about self-determination and sovereignty. But, being a philosopher, I am going to get there by a roundabout route.

AGAINST PHILOSOPHY: UNTHEORIZED AGREEMENTS

Philosophy, I said, is kibitzing plus attending to the big picture.

To attend to the big picture, let me say first of all, is not necessarily to insist on philosophical or metaphysical foundations. It seems to me, as it does to Michael Ignatieff and did to the drafters of the Universal Declaration, that it is an important advantage of international humanitarian law that it does not proceed by deriving human rights from metaphysical first principles. These laws do not say—as the American Declaration of Independence did—that our rights flow from our being created equal (which presupposes, of course, that we were created at all). I think that it is an advantage because human rights as they actually exist are, above all, creatures of something like law: they are the results of agreements promulgated by states, agreements that set rule-governed constraints on the actions of states and individuals, sometimes requiring action, sometimes forbidding it. They are used by officials to justify actions both within and across states, and they are called upon by citizens of many states claiming protection from abuse. The wide diversity of people who call upon them includes, as Michael Ignatieff rightly insists, a substantial diversity of opinion on matters metaphysical—on religion in particular—and even if there is a single truth to be had about these matters, it is not one that we shall all come to soon.

What lay behind the thinking of those who first developed the European liberal doctrines of human rights—I am thinking here of seventeenth- and eighteenth-century theorists—was, in part, the history of barbarous religious warfare within Western Christendom, and the conviction that, since people could not be forced into religious conformity, we were going to have to learn to live with religious differences. Now these earlier documents were nevertheless still framed within a Christian order: Locke did not think that it made sense to extend toleration to atheists (in part because he thought only theists could be trusted to keep oaths that they had sworn). Nevertheless, they began to acknowledge (what had long been acknowledged under Muslim law) that communities of different faiths ought to be allowed to practice their religions, within certain limits, even in states where one particular faith was established.

The major advantage of instruments that are not framed as the working out of a metaphysical tradition is, obviously, that people from different metaphysical traditions can accept them. The major disadvantage is that without some grounding—metaphysical or not—it is hard to see why they should have any power or effect. The mere making of declarations that one should behave this way or that does not in general lead people to act in conformity with them, especially in the absence of mechanisms of enforcement. So, granted that they are so weakly philosophically grounded, there is a puzzle about what gives human rights instruments their power.

The answer, I think, is implicit in Michael Ignatieff's remark that "[h]uman rights has gone global by going local." People around the world, working in different religious and juridical traditions, have nevertheless found reasons to support various human rights instruments because those instruments embody protections that they both want and need. We do not need to agree that we are all created in the image of God, or that we have natural rights that flow from our human essence, to agree that we do not want to be tortured by government officials, that we do not want our lives, families, and property forfeited. And ordinary people almost everywhere have something like the notion of dignity—it has different names and somewhat different configurations in different places—and desire something like respect from their fellows and believe that they merit it unless they do evil. From these diverse roots, enthusiasm for many human rights has grown. In effect, for many of our human rights, the reason why we do not need to ground them in any particular metaphysics is that they are already grounded in many metaphysics and can already derive sustenance from those many sources.

A simple example, which I have used before, can come from the traditions of Asante, where I grew up. Free As-

ante citizens—both men and women—in the period before our state was conquered by Britain, as well as since,
are preoccupied with notions of personal dignity, with respect and self-respect. Treating others with the respect
that is their due is a central preoccupation of Asante social life, as is a reciprocal anxiety about loss of respect,
shame, and disgrace. Just as European liberalism—and
democratic sentiment—grew by extending to every man
and (then) woman the dignity that feudal society offered
only to the aristocracy, and thus presupposes, in some
sense, aspects of that feudal understanding of dignity, so
modern Ghanaian thinking about politics depends, in
part, on the prior grasp of concepts such as *animuonyam*
(respect). It is clear from well-known Akan proverbs that
respect was precisely not something that belonged in the
past to everybody:

> *Agya Kra ne Agya Kwakyereme, emu biara mu nni ani-
> muonyam.* (Father Soul and Father Slave Kyereme,
> neither is respected; that is, whatever you call him, a
> slave is still a slave.)

But just as *dignitas*, which was once, by definition, the
property of an elite, has grown into human dignity, which
is the property of every man and woman, so *animuonyam*
can be the basis of the respect for all others that lies at
the heart of a commitment to human rights.

When it comes to those cases where the different traditions part, a metaphysical grounding would not help us.
For when someone argues that the human rights tradition is too individualist, and so that certain individual
rights have a lesser weight than community interests, and
argues in the name of Confucian values or Maoism or

Hinduism or Islam, the return to first principles will simply take us from one terrain of disagreement to another where there seems no reason to expect greater hope of resolution.

In a recent Tanner Lecture, Cass Sunstein defended the notion of "incompletely theorized agreements" in American constitutional law.[1] What I am defending here is a similar freedom from high doctrine in the development of the international law of human rights: we should be able to defend our treaties by arguing that they offer people protections against governments that most of their citizens desire—protections important enough that they also want other peoples, through their governments, to help sustain them. Once we seek to defend these rights in this pragmatic way, we can appeal to a very diverse set of arguments: perhaps some rights—to freedom of expression, for example—are not only necessary for dignity and the maintenance of respect but also helpful in the development of economies and the stabilization of polities. And all of these are things that are wanted by most people everywhere.

To say this is to make a point that is exactly a pragmatic one. It is not to say that the legitimizing foundation of human rights is the consent of a majority of our species. And so it is not, in particular, to agree with the position attributed to most Americans by Paul Kahn, as Michael cites him, to the effect that rights acquire their legitimacy from the consent of the governed. I do not think this is a coherent idea because our most fundamental rights restrain majorities, and their consent to the system that embodies those restraints does not entail their consent to the rights themselves—otherwise there would be no need of them. If consent is an empirical notion, then most Americans do not consent to many rights that we actually have: the right, for example, even if we are condemned for capital crimes, to marry. The point about widespread assent that I am making is only that we can understand much of the success of human rights talk as a reflection of the fact that it speaks to people in a wide diversity of positions and traditions, and that, because of that chord of resonating agreement, we can find support for the human rights system in many, many places. Part of the point of articulating these ideas in international documents, widely circulated and advertised, is just to draw attention to that core of agreement and help to give it practical force. Since human rights can be sustained in these ways without metaphysical debate, and since metaphysical debate is unlikely to yield consensus, let us proceed to endorse and enforce them without it as much as we can.

What I have just said is a point about what sort of fact the first key fact is. And I want to underscore a crucial point that Michael Ignatieff makes. Simply put, the spread of human rights culture and the growth of human rights NGOs all around the world does not amount to the diffusion of a metaphysics of Enlightenment liberalism. To the extent that that is right, we do not have to defend it against the charge of ethnocentrism.

Methodological Individualism

I should now like to make a general point about the second key fact: the fact that there is the possibility of practical conflict between individual rights and state sovereignty. At a number of cruxes in his argument, Michael

Ignatieff raises questions about balancing the rights of individuals against the demands of various collectivities. He also mentions cases where what is at stake are competing collectivities—Serbs and Albanian Kossovars, Turks and Kurds, even, several times, Americans, on the one hand, and the international community (or perhaps just Europeans), on the other. In the face of the issues raised here, he seems both inclined to make concessions toward one sort of collectivity—the nation-state—and to be wary about acknowledging the desire for self-determination on the part of others—such as the Kosovars or the Timorese.

I confess to sharing these instincts: I am skeptical about acceding too much to subnational groups, even, as he is, skeptical about rights to self-determination that are already supposedly embedded in international law; and I am a lukewarm enthusiast, as he is too, for the nation-state and for civil rights associated with location rather than ancestry. And I think it is easy enough to see why we are both likely to be unsympathetic to such views. Michael Ignatieff is a Canadian of Eastern European ancestry educated at Harvard and living in London. In a moment I am going to discuss the work of a Ugandan intellectual of Asian ancestry who was his roommate at Harvard: a man who has just moved from the University of Cape Town to Columbia University. I am an Anglo-Ghanaian, born in London, raised in Ghana, living in Boston. The week before I delivered the original version of these remarks, I traveled down from Kumasi, in Ghana, to Accra, the capital, in a car in which the languages were Japanese, English and Asante-Twi, with a young man whom I have known since he was an infant, because we grew up on the same street, who now lives partly with his Japanese wife just outside Tokyo. The last time Michael and I met (before the lectures that form the basis of his essays in this volume) was at a Catholic university in Brabant in Holland, a country we here think of as the ur-Protestant society. We—he and I—are exactly the kinds of world travelers whom our enemies think of as "rootless cosmopolitans," lacking the authentic rooted group identities that claim collective rights: we are people who have no use for group rights ourselves because our own movements across the boundaries of states require the protection of our individualities, not the acknowledgment of our groups.

I think that people like us have a special responsibility to resist these inclinations we share because of the kinds of lives we share, and to try to engage with some sympathy with the claims of groups that are not of much use to *us*. This is in keeping with the generally pragmatic approach I urged at the start: let's see what kind of case for group rights as a legal practice might meet the interests and the needs of actual people in a way that might generate consensus on endorsing those protections in international instruments.

Before proceeding with those questions, however, I think it will be helpful to make two distinctions: one about individualism and one about group rights. The distinction about individualism in the sphere of rights is between what I will call methodological individualism and substantive individualism. Methodological individualism about rights I thoroughly endorse. It is the view that we should defend rights by showing what they do for individuals—social individuals, to be sure, living in families and communities, usually, but still individuals. Substantive individualism about rights is the view that rights must always attach to individuals: that human rights, as framed in our conventions and in law, should always be the rights of persons, not of groups. It is substantive individualism that I am going to ask us to interrogate. We can then take up my first point—that rights are fundamentally creatures of law—and ask what laws, including what laws assigning rights to groups, would be good for individuals.

But that interrogation can proceed usefully only if we make a second distinction: that between two ways of thinking of group rights. One is to think of them as exercised collectively: for this to work in practice, there have to be mechanisms by which the groups can be legally identified and institutions through which their interests can be asserted. If an American Indian tribe has the collective right to run a gaming casino, it must be decided both who belongs to that tribe and how they should decide whether to exercise the right. The right of self-determination is a group right of this sort, and it raises both kinds of questions. Who is a Palestinian, a Kurd, a Tibetan? And how should they decide to exercise their rights? Call group rights of this sort *collective rights*.

A second conception of group rights is the idea that the law, whether national or international, might treat each member of certain groups as being individually entitled to certain claims qua member of the group. For example, each member of the English hereditary peerage used to be able to exercise the right to a trial by the House of Lords. Call group rights of this sort *membership rights*.

Membership rights are individual rights in a certain sense: they belong to individuals. But those who say they are skeptical of group rights often mean to be challenging membership rights. What they are objecting to is the idea that a state should relate to any citizen in virtue of his or her membership in a group rather than simply as a citizen. It was an objection to the membership rights of whites (and the membership burdens of blacks) that underlay much of the opposition to American Jim Crow and to apartheid. The only membership rights that have a large body of support are the membership rights of citizens of democratic states: it is widely thought to be fine to treat citizens and noncitizens differently before the law, for example, in deciding who may take jobs where.

Collective rights tend to have more friends, however. Most people think that it is just fine that Utah or the city of Cambridge or the Catholic Church can exercise rights, through the ballot box or (in the case of churches) through whatever consensual internal mechanisms they agree upon.

RIGHTS, RACE, CUSTOM

I was lucky to hear a talk by that roommate of Michael Ignatieff's from Uganda the day before I was to reply to the Tanner Lectures on which Michael's essays here are based. His name is Mahmood Mamdani. (Given the quality of their lectures, I wish I could have been a fly on the wall on that room at Harvard!) Mahmood Mamdani was talking about the legacies of colonialism in African states. Roughly, the picture was this: the colonial state divided people into two categories. There were citizens, who had races (White, Indian, Arab), civil rights, and a separation of powers under the rule of law; then there were subjects, who had tribes, under customary law, and a chief who had been turned into a despot, through the ignoring of the different corporate sources of power (age sets, clans, etc.) of the precolonial order. Membership in tribes was decided by suppositiously traditional means, and which tribal jurisdiction you came under depended on what tribe you belonged to, not on where you were living. If you combine custom with the idea of indigeneity, as happened in British indirect-rule customary law, you get not only membership rights but also exactly the sorts of discrimination between individuals that leads to skepticism about membership rights. Migrant labor, traders, capitalists, all of whom move across customary jurisdictions, end up having no customary status; and if you assign special rights to people qua members of tribes, you end up discriminating against the nonindigene: thus the Banyamulenge in Congo are "really" Rwandese Tutsis and so must leave; the Igbo traders in northern Nigeria are really easterners and so may be killed; the Asian capitalists, large and small, in Uganda are really members of no tribe and so can settle nowhere.[2]

One obvious suggestion here is to tie rights not to indigeneity but to residence, but to allow that this will mean that some minority residents of some regions will be governed in part by standards they do not think of as authentically theirs.

Listening to Mahmood Madmdani talk, I was bound to reflect on my own experience of custom, especially since I had just returned from spending a week participating in the final funeral rites of the late king of Asante and talking to the new king about his ambitions for putting his own position to positive use.[3]

This is not the place to say in detail how I think we should deal with the problem that Mahmood Mamdani raised for Africa's inheritance of the framework of customary law. But it provides a good example of the sorts of questions we have to answer if we are to think sensibly both about group rights as collective rights, the right of the Asante to continue their kingship within the Ghanaian republic, and about membership rights—the possession by Asante indigenes, however defined, to land rights that are not held by others. What I have been suggesting is that in thinking about such questions as matters of international human rights law—for example, "Is the persistence of Asante customary law consistent with the human rights of non-Asante Ghanaians resident in the Asante region?"—we should be guided by two thoughts.

First: we should ask what features of the international regime can be "taken local" by allowing people and peoples to see that they have interests that can be served by the institutionalization of those rights.

Second: if collective and membership rights are urged, they should be evaluated, in the same way, by our asking whether they would be good, on balance, in the actual circumstances, for individuals.

In sum I want to defend the utility of human rights as practical instruments for serving human purposes, for that way we can gather, I believe, a greater consensus behind them; I am open to group legal rights—both membership and collective—but only as instruments in the service of enriching the lives and the possibilities of individuals. Since taking human rights local and a preference for individual over collective rights are both features of

Michael Ignatieff's proposals in these essays, I hope that these will be seen by him—and by everyone—as friendly elaborations of some of the themes he has so helpfully begun to set before us.

NOTES

1. Cass R. Sunstein, "Political Conflict and Legal Agreement," in *The Tanner Lectures on Human Values*, vol. 17, ed. Grethe B. Peterson (Salt Lake City: University of Utah Press, 1996), p. 137.

2. These issues are discussed in Mahmood Mamdani's book *Citizen and Subject* (Princeton: Princeton University Press, 1996).

3. I discuss these issues further in "Context in Political Philosophy," in *Explorations in African Political Thought: Identity, Community, Ethics*, ed. Teodros Kiros (New York: Routledge, 2000), pp. 45–53.

Debates with the PTA and Others

DAVID A. HOLLINGER

IF I WERE a patriarchal, theocratic authoritarian, an official of a sovereign nation-state organized in relation to a traditional culture, eager to use the technologies of the West but equally eager to avoid social and political liberalization, I would be very suspicious of Michael Ignatieff. I'd say to him something like the following. You, Ignatieff, claim that you don't have designs on the entirety of my culture, so long as folks can leave it when they wish. You say that your human rights agenda is limited to providing the basis for what you call "any life whatever," and that you imagine many different kinds of social goods in a culturally plural world. You imply that you expect my culture to continue pretty much unchanged except that we have to stop killing our women when they dishonor us men. But you do not understand the extent to which my culture is defined by the very things you are against. And you do not understand that the liberals in my midst, whom you like to cite as examples of the diversity of my own tradition, are selling out to the West, are profaning the faith of their fathers by using the name of this faith as a cover for de facto Western liberal ideas, and are undercutting the political culture of our state by seeking to introduce a free press, by trying to weaken the civic role of our ecclesiastical authorities, and by asking that we educate our women. These sellouts are your cultural colonials, Ignatieff, who are of use to you because of their own continued, public affiliation with my religion and my state and my culture; they make it seem that your project is directed not against us but only against what you imply is one part of us. You thus divide us and potentially conquer us by encouraging these liberals not only to liberalize but to liberalize within our tradition rather than by renouncing it and owning up to their adoption of foreign, ultimately Western values. And the difficulty of separating out your ostensibly minimalist human rights agenda from the larger project of liberalization is shown by the fact that your human rights agenda gets the most support within my society from these same liberals, these same sellouts. Hence you, Ignatieff, are more subversive than you allow. You acknowledge that my society has divisions within in, but you are taking sides, supporting the subversives and opposing me and my kind. You seem to be willing to accept the continuation of my way of life, but the sharp distinction you draw between a minimalist human rights agenda and a more wholesale transformation of culture and politics in individualist, egalitarian directions will not stand up: your human rights agenda is a slippery slope, a foot in the door, the camel's nose in the tent—you can pick your figure of speech. You remind me of those American liberals in the 1950s and early 1960s who said that the end of segregation would not mean intermarriage, but in 1967 the Supreme Court ruled unconstitutional the laws of Virginia and other states prohibiting interracial marriage, and now such marriages are increasing, especially in the military, where the atmosphere of a secular civic government is the least confined by local custom. So while you now disaggregate basic human rights from the more sweeping individualism, egalitarianism, and democratic political culture so often associated with human rights, and while you tell even members of your own tribe that human rights is just a tool kit and not part of a more ambitious program of global reform, I as an old-fashioned patriarchal, theocratic authoritarian see through your designs. I will not be deceived into putting at risk my culture, my patriarchy, my theocracy, my authority, just to satisfy the demand for what you call minimal human rights.

But fortunately for Ignatieff, and even more fortunately for me, I am not a patriarchal, theocratic authoritarian. I take on this fictional persona in order to bring out several of the issues raised by Ignatieff's approach to human rights theory. Two such issues are, first, the viability of the distinction between a minimalist human rights program and the larger matrix of Enlightenment aspirations out of which the human rights program as understood in the North Atlantic West has emerged, and, second, the boundaries of the moral community being invited to accept this distinction, and to accept Ignatieff's overall justification for human rights. The complaints of our patriarchal, theocratic authoritarian—whom I will henceforth flag with the acronym PTA, reminding us incidentally of the often conservative cultural concerns of some groups closer to home—illustrate the first of these two issues more vividly than the second. But the second issue, too, comes into view when we decide how seriously to take the PTA's opinions. Just whom is Ignatieff trying to persuade? Does he—do we who sympathize with his endeavor and share the dilemmas on which his essays are so refreshingly forthright and resourceful a commentary—care about the PTA except as a strategic matter? Is our own confidence in the human rights project diminished because of the objections raised by the PTA?

Before I comment on these two issues, I want to acknowledge that it is a struggle for me to find much to argue with in Ignatieff's essays. I find myself so appreciative of his exemplary good sense, his cautious theoretical refinements, his candid secularism, and his ability to take account of context-specific constraints and possibilities, that I invoke the alien persona of the PTA by way of getting into the critical mode. Ignatieff is, to my knowledge, unique in his ability to address simultaneously and effectively the concerns of both human rights activists and human rights theorists. His example stands as a commanding rebuke to those activists who regard theory as little more than an invitation to be precious and divisive, and a rebuke, also, to those theorists who find the historical particularity of the activist's daily work to be an irrelevant distraction. The great value of Michael Ignatieff's essays is not the basic justification for human rights that he articulates, excellent as that justification is. The great value of these essays is, rather, the model they provide for deliberation in human rights matters, for taking a variety of considerations into account in relation to every human rights decision, for patiently staying with the project even though victory is rarely in sight.

In regard to the first of the two issues—the viability of so sharp a distinction between a minimalist human rights program and that program's broader matrix of Enlightenment aspirations—I want to note parenthetically that when I invoke the concept of the Enlightenment, I do not imply that the North Atlantic West has a monopoly on humane ideas. Anthony Appiah has reminded us of the multiple sources for some of the ideas that are sometimes presented as the simple diffusion of European culture. Yet Appiah also points out, wisely, in his important essay "Cosmopolitan Patriots,"[1] that no idea should be discredited because the idea happened to come to someone from the European Enlightenment. Most people who live in the North Atlantic West did get their human rights sensitivity in the context of the Enlightenment, and in the context of the Christian universalism with which the Enlightenment has been so deeply entangled. Hence I, like Ignatieff, employ the term "Enlightenment" as historical shorthand.

I note that Ignatieff himself points frequently to this Enlightenment matrix. "[O]nly Western culture," he observes, "turned widely shared propositions about human dignity and equality into a working doctrine of rights." But if this doctrine "originated not in Djeddah or Beijing," as Ignatieff observes, is it likely that the Djeddahs and Beijings of our time can take the doctrine without any of the sustaining cultural conditions that developed historically alongside it? Isn't the PTA on to something? Don't we want human rights to be a slippery slope toward democracy and the rule of law? Isn't it simply true that human rights abuses are more likely to occur in nations lacking the consent of the governed, lacking democracy? Must we not grant the point of those in the human rights community who argue that a human rights agenda is, willy-nilly, connected to an international politics that would promote the social, cultural, and political conditions conducive to the diminution of cruelty?

Ignatieff cites Amartya Sen to the effect that human rights are important as a stepping-stone toward a more general human welfare. Minimal human rights, followed by a free press and democratic government, maximize the opportunity that a society will avoid the calamity of China's Great Leap Forward. If the PTA read this part of Ignatieff's essay, the ambitious liberal reforming cat would surely be out of the human rights minimalist bag. And I wonder what percentage of the pro-human-rights constituencies in China, Indonesia, or Algeria today are eager to renounce the hope of democracy and the rule of law? If there is good reason to believe that human rights can serve as a vanguard for democracy, why, other than strategic necessity, should we be quiet about this prospect? Strategic minimalism makes good sense strategically, but it carries the same risk carried by its famous sibling, strategic essentialism: the risk that it shall deceive its own advocates.

This uncertainty about the relation of strategic minimalism to what we really think brings us to the question of just whom one wants to persuade. Ignatieff presents the "spiritual" crisis of human rights as internal to "us," but he seems to regard this crisis as the result, at least in part, of our taking seriously the sensibilities of people like the PTA. The minimalism of Ignatieff's theory of human rights, his divestment of one argument after another until we are finally reduced to a variation on the Golden Rule—"the basic intuition," as he puts in his concluding paragraph, "that what is pain and humiliation for you is bound to be pain and humiliation for me"—follows importantly from the range of the perspectives he wants to satisfy. Arguments with greater density, arguments that exploit the historically particular intellectual and moral traditions sharpened within the West against the West's own propensity for murder, these arguments, Ignatieff ruefully discards. In so doing, Ignatieff reenacts in our time the drama of 1947 and 1948 that he so sensitively recounts: the silencing of certain ideas in order to render one's formulations acceptable in a larger and more diverse community. Yet the drafters of the Universal Declaration were trying to create a document that would be signed by sovereign states, all of them, if possible; hence the demands of strategic minimalism were implacable. These demands need not be quite so controlling of a theory designed to motivate and mobilize a constituency smaller than the entire United Nations.

I wonder whether Ignatieff's strategic minimalism has not exercised too much influence over the terms on which he tries to convince himself and others in his own tribe of the soundness of the human rights endeavor. My fear is that Ignatieff, despite his open and robust affirmation of individualism, despite his pointed complaint that human rights activists have conceded too much to cultural relativism, is himself too eager to get the PTA's assent, too willing to scale back his justification of human rights so that even the PTA might find that justification cogent and convincing. Perhaps we can more readily convince ourselves that we are right if we admit that the world is indeed so plural, culturally, that not everyone can be brought to accept even the Golden Rule? Perhaps the spiritual crisis of human rights can be more easily resolved if we scale back not our theory of human rights but the circle of people whom we want to persuade of that theory's validity?

Such a turn would seem fully consistent with Ignatieff's welcome willingness to justify human rights in terms that will not satisfy those for whom theism is indispensable. The religious and the secular subcommunities of our tribe can develop their own variations on human rights theory without getting in each other's way. Ignatieff seems not to object to religious belief as a basis for human rights so long as those who accept that basis will refrain from foisting it upon the rest of us, telling us, their secular allies, that without God we have no sound theory of human rights. Ignatieff wisely does not try to persuade religionists to give up their religious foundation for human rights.

So, too, might Ignatieff loosen up a bit on the children of the Enlightenment. I do not find the statements by Elie Wiesel, Kofi Annan, and Nadine Gordimer nearly as troubling as Ignatieff does. These utterances are hyperbolic, but exaggeration is not idolatry. When these figures use terms like "religion" and "creed" to talk about human rights, I read them in the same way I read Ignatieff when he describes human rights as a tool kit: all are using figures of speech. Our choice of metaphors is significant, but when Ignatieff elaborates on agency and negative liberty and individualism, what he says might well strike someone else as a creed of sorts. The principle of individual agency is not so modest, given the extent and depth of the forces arrayed against such agency. Ignatieff does a terrific job developing a nonidolatrous theory of human rights, but the strength of his theory is somewhat obscured by his presenting it primarily as an alternative to idolatry. Rights inflation may be unwise for all the reasons Ignatieff gives, but there may be room for a bit of thickness in secular as well as religious justifications for human rights. The danger is not so much that we will all be stampeded into accepting too thick a justification of human rights, but that we will diminish the size and energy of the human rights community by rendering unwelcome in it some people who join because of theories that neither Ignatieff nor I—my own secular sentiments are very much like his—can accept.

Why do I think we need to keep more open than Ignatieff does the door for people with thick theories of human rights? Because we need all the help we can get. As we develop awareness, thanks partly to Ignatieff's writings here and elsewhere, of how frustrating human rights activities become, of how complex are the politics of human rights, of how truly difficult it is to get anything done right, the more we may need the confidence in the human rights endeavor that thick theories can provide. The challenge may be less to develop a single minimalist theory of human rights than to coordinate the activities of people motivated by several somewhat thicker theories, and to connect the common denominator of these theories to the actual politics of the world. No one has done more than Ignatieff to show us how this can be done. But if the religious are to be granted their Yahweh and their Christ, their Ten Commandments and their Sermon on the Mount, then we secularists should be allowed our Locke and our Rous-

seau, our Dewey and our Habermas, our Thomas Jefferson and our Elizabeth Cady Stanton.

Note

1. Kwame Anthony Appiah, "Cosmopolitan Patriots," *Critical Inquiry* 23 (Spring 1997): 617–39.

The Moral Imagination and Human Rights

THOMAS W. LAQUEUR

MICHAEL IGNATIEFF begins his first essay with an incident reported by Primo Levi in *If This Is a Man*: Levi is standing opposite the chief of the chemical department at Auschwitz. His life depends on convincing this erstwhile colleague that he—Levi—is a competent chemist and hence more useful to the camp alive than dead. He remembers that Dr. Pannwitz, the man on the other side of the desk, stared up at him with a "look [that] was not one between two men . . . [a look] which came as if across the glass window of an aquarium between two beings who live in different worlds." If, Levi says, he could have explained the nature of that look—one not between two humans beings but—to take the metaphor literally—between a human being and some other, in this case, aquatic species, one might explain "the essence of the great insanity of the third German [reich]." A least one form of moral progress, Ignatieff suggests, consists in the degree to which "we act upon the moral intuition that Dr. Pannwitz was wrong" and, conversely, subscribe to the view that "our species is one, and each of the individuals who compose it is entitled to moral equal consideration." Progress in this sense is nothing more, or less, than the global diffusion of the Golden Rule—the expansion of the species category "human" as the bearer of a moral franchise— into ever expanding spheres.

There is, however, a second and perhaps more mundane sense of moral progress to which Ignatieff turns immediately: that is, progress as the increasing acceptance of "human *rights* instruments." This is a juridical development; the emphasis here is less on "human" than on "rights." Its history begins, of course, in the Enlightenment and finds its first great legal articulation in the French Revolutionary "Declaration of the Rights of Man and Citizen." There are foreshadowings of what would become an international human rights before the late twentieth century: one thinks of the legal foundations of the nineteenth-century suppression of the slave trade and of the ineffective noises made in protest against the Armenian massacres. But there were no actual covenants or treaties guaranteeing group or individual rights. Ignatieff is right to begin with the slow but steady climb out of the near collapse of European civilization in 1945. A jurisprudential revolution was meant to guarantee "Never again." Before 1948 only states had internationally recognized rights; in that year—a sort of ground zero—the Universal Declaration of Human Rights granted such rights to individuals threatened by states or by oppressive customary practices, that is, by communities. In 1948, too, the Genocide Convention protected the *rights* of religious, racial, and ethnic groups threatened by persecution or extermination; the next year, 1949, the Geneva Convention guaranteeing noncombatant immunity was strengthened; in 1951 came conventions protecting the *rights* of refugees. Finally, in 1953 the European Convention on Human Rights. And, of course, there are various national histories—the progress of the civil *rights* movement in the United States, for example. Progress in this second sense is expansion of rights based in law rather than in fellow feeling.

And finally, there is the history of moral progress as the history of the advocacy revolution and the advent of institutions to punish human rights offenders. Those whose rights have been trampled are no longer alone; the state's monopoly on international affairs has been broken, and literally hundreds of organizations watch for human rights abuses by whoever might commit them. War criminals and perpetrators of genocide are on trial as we speak.

But this triumphalist story is incomplete. Why is there a deep sense of perplexity and discouragement among human rights activists at the very same time that human rights language seems to be everywhere. Why, to put it differently, would any one of us not be tempted to demur from the first part of Ignatieff's essay by simply offering a list: a million civilians dead, tortured, bombed, or displaced here, maybe two million there, 500,000 or 100,000, maybe only tens of thousands somewhere else; India and Pakistan; Biafra; El Salvador and Nicaragua and the bombing of civilians in Vietnam, to get closer to home; the dirty war in the Argentine; Pinochet's Chile; Cambodia; Palestine; Algeria, both during its war with France and during its war with itself; Bosnia; Croatia; Kosovo; Rwanda; Chechnya. Where is moral progress here? It is tempting, as Ignatieff says, to let this catalog answer for itself: we are disappointed with what the international human rights movement has achieved because abuses increase faster than our ability to stop them.

But he offers a different answer. Human rights activism has been insatiable in its demands and insatiably disappointed because it fails to define the limits of its reach. With a horizonless view of the potential of the human rights movement and of the efficacy of military and other forms of intervention, we in the West have put the legitimacy of the rights standard itself into question and in some situations have even made bad situations worse. These essays thus articulate limits—first of all, on the circumstances under which the human rights movement and the governments it influences will impinge on the sovereignty of states and, specifically, use military force to right some wrong: the limits of intervention, in other words. It is justifiable only in such cases where all standards or fairness and the protection of the individual have collapsed—where negative liberty is in serious jeopardy—and not in all those cases in which a particular Western standard of democracy and political openness is not met.

At the heart of Ignatieff's position—governing his account both of moral progress and of a politics of intervention—is the point that he makes near the end of his first essay: that "legitimate institutions . . . alone are the best guarantee of human rights protection." I think this is a terribly important, and well-taken, point—but I do not think that it rests either in a history of the universalization of the species category "human" designating a moral subject, or in the history of moral progress as the universalization of "rights."

Put differently, Ignatieff's fundamental point is that it is an error to rely for the protection of human rights on the conversion of the world's people and governments to a set of universal principles. We should strive instead to expand the writ of constitutional guarantees for individual self-determination: constitutional guarantees of negative liberty. If this is the case, the problem may not be so much a matter of learning to consider some *distant* creatures as human and hence worthy of decent treatment. Nor is it primarily one of articulating the conditions under which one might want to protect others when such treatment is not forthcoming, that is, developing an international politics of intervention. We must, rather, create the conditions under which our fellow humans treat their *neighbors* as themselves, developing local political cultures that protect individual liberties.

In this context, I want to suggest two alternative histories that arrive at much the same place as does Ignatieff. In so doing, I do not want to detract from his emphasis on the revolution in world politics that the post-1948 rights revolution has wrought. But I do think that the possibility of a world in which legitimate institutions protect individuals from tyranny, death, and oppression depends on historically quite specific conditions of local political culture that deserve attention. I do not want to suggest that cultural understanding will protect anyone; there is little evidence for this and much to the contrary. But I do want to propose that the sort of constitutionalism Ignatieff proposes is grounded in specific, historically rich, political conditions.

Let me begin with the history of the "intuition that Dr. Pannwitz was wrong." It is a history of the expansion less of the category "human" than of the moral imagination that allows us to regard the suffering of distant humans as making the same sort of claim on us as the suffering of proximate ones. The imperative to treat those outside of one's intimate circle humanely is, of course—as Ignatieff has written elsewhere (*The Needs of Strangers*)—a long-standing one. "Love the sojourner therefore, for you were sojourners in the land of Egypt" (Deut. 10:18–19). "I was a stranger and you welcomed me" (Matt. 25:35), Jesus said, in the context of telling his disciples that any act of kindness to another human in need is an act of kindness toward him. "Humanities is the general name given to those virtues in whom seemeth to be a general concorde and love in the nature of man," says Sir Thomas Elyot, the author of the first English work on moral philosophy, in 1531.[1]

Humane behavior in this sense entailed neither a universal abstract theory of right nor a commitment to human equality—social or juridical. Clearly acts of charity, hospitality, and courtesy were as often practiced by social superiors to their inferiors as to their equals or superiors. Indeed, in an aristocratic society such acts of humanity were meant to produce the nexus of hierarchically ordered attachments, mutual obligations, and rewards that constituted the social order predicated on inequality. Efforts to expand the domain of obligation must begin with the recognition that in the first instances humanity was local—autarchic. Those who mattered were those who were close and already connected.

The history that Ignatieff points to as beginning with the antislavery movement constitutes the story of the unlikely—in some instances even undesirable—reversal of what appears so natural: the story of how the suffering of distant strangers came to matter as much as one's own suffering or that of one's near and dear. This is Diderot's Chinese mandarin problem.[2] It is an extraordinary demand that Adam Smith understood with fine precision: "If he were to lose his little finger to-morrow," he says, he "would not sleep to-night. But, provided he never saw them, he will snore with the most profound security over the ruin of a hundred millions of his brethren, and the destruction of that immense multitude seems plainly an object less interesting to him, than this paltry misfortune of his own."[3] And two centuries later, after Auschwitz, it is echoed by Primo Levi:

> If we were able to suffer the sufferings of everyone, we could not live. Perhaps the dreadful gift of pity for many is granted only to saints. . . . and to all of us there remains in the best of cases only the sporadic pity addressed to the single individual, the Mitmensch, the co-man: the human being of flesh and blood standing before us, within the reach of our providentially myopic senses.[4]

Humanity for Diderot, Smith, Primo Levi—and, indeed, most of us—in the first instance begins at home.

The question then becomes, How is distant suffering to become the equivalent of suffering at home? And the answer that began to be articulated in the late seventeenth century and is repeated every day as we see documentaries about Rwanda, or photographs of mass graves in Bosnia, or of starving children in the Sudan, is that "the soul expands herself abroad, and finds that she is actually related to all surrounding beings," to use Nicolas Malebranche's metaphor.[5] Something—a faculty and some stimulus to that faculty—allows us to reach out; something that by the eighteenth century was construed to be a natural sympathy. Perhaps, as William Wollaston argued in the 1720s, "human nature" was constituted with a generic disposition that "renders us obnoxious to the pains of others, causes us to sympathize with them, and almost comprehends us in their case." For Wollaston this disposition is almost physiological; our reaction is direct and in response, it seems, to an actual, present distress: "[I]t is grievous to hear (and almost to hear of) any man, or even any animal whatever, in torment."[6]

It is precisely this sense of immediate local sympathy that came to be expanded through what we might call the moral imagination, the capacity to somehow feel the exigency of wrongs suffered by strangers at a distance. As Adam Smith most famously argued, the imagination brings the outer world in:

> By the imagination we place ourselves in his situation, we conceive ourselves enduring all the same torments, we enter as it were into his body, and become in some measure the same person with him, and thence form some idea of his sensations. . . . His agonies, when they are thus brought home to ourselves, when we have thus adopted and made them our own, begin at last to affect us, and then we tremble and shudder at the thought of what he feels.[7]

Thus images and words substitute for the sound of the cry, for the sight of blood and mangled flesh, for the look of suffering.

In an important sense this story has reached its de-nouement. Today technologies of all sorts bring the hu-man rights abuses of the whole wide world home, and we seem to have no difficulty in encompassing—at least on occasion—all of humanity within the fold of our compas-sion. Successors to the economic boycotts of the 1790s against sugar have become commonplace as we eschew all sorts of products produced under bad conditions in much of the Third World. The British efforts to restrict the world slave trade were but the first instance of an international politics of human rights that—as Ignatieff has told us—now enjoys center stage.

The difficulty now is not that of regarding a stranger as a fellow human and thus worthy of moral regard: it is, rather, that in much of the world *intimates* treat one an-other badly. As Elaine Scarry has argued in *The Body in Pain*, much of the most horrible violence of the past de-cades has been directed against those closest to the per-petrators—civil, not international, conflict. Not sur-prisingly, perhaps, the abstract "human" is easier to cherish and respect than the all-too-real creature next door. In one sense this may seem to be the dilemma of Dickens's Mrs. Jelleby, who cares so deeply for the chil-dren of some obscure African country while her own chil-dren run wild. But not quite. Her children did not mur-der one another.

The historical question I should like to put to Ig-natieff's account of the politics of human rights is the following: Under what conditions are differences—devia-tions of various sorts from cultural norms, from dominant political or religious or sexual beliefs and practices—tol-erated and regarded as compatible with civilization and with civilized conduct, and under what circumstances are they not? It seems to me that the extraordinary feature of so many contemporary abuses of human rights—and of their earlier historical forms under whatever name—is that almost in an instant one group seems to find another not merely objectionable, wrong, inferior, or even hostile but so deeply antithetical not just to this or that civilization but to the very idea of civilization itself as to be unworthy of life. And then, quite dramatically, the threat seems to vanish.

In some cases, of course, the object of such repugnance is successfully destroyed. Clearly the very existence of native Americans in California was thought to be incompatible with modern life, and genocide did not end until all but the tiniest handful of Indians were left alive. But this is not the only resolution. In European history one might ask the question in the form posed by J. H. Plumb in his account of the rise of political stability in England: why did rulers and other public servants, and, by extension, their subjects, come to die in bed and not at the stake or the block or in fratricidal war?[8] (One does not want to push this too far, as one remembers the Scottish Highlands and Ireland.) Another obvious case might be the French Wars of Religion. On August 23–24, 1572, some six thousand Protestants in Paris were murdered in all manner of brutal ways. Proportionately this would be the equivalent of nearly a third of a million people murdered in one night in New York or Los Angeles. There followed more murder in the provinces and several decades of fratricidal war. And the denouement: a legal decree of toleration by a king strong enough to enforce it;

the institutional protection of individual rights. A strong state to the rescue, to use, somewhat anachronistically, Ignatieff's point about sovereignty in his first essay.

His second essay argues that one needs only a thin theory of rights—a commitment to the protection of the individual, the idea of negative liberty—to accomplish such an end. But perhaps we do not need a universalistic notion of rights at all to protect the individual; historically rooted, or other so-called traditional liberties and restraints, might do. Hermann Hesse, reflecting on the Great War, remarked that it had "destroyed and lost for the greater part of the civilized world . . . beyond all else, the two universal foundations of life, culture and morality: religion and customary morals." What is gone, he said, is a "traditional, sacred, unwritten understanding about what is proper and becoming between people."[9] Maybe not just religion and customary morals, but certainly something other than a universal precept. What divides the two sides in the fratricidal war in Sri Lanka is not varying views of human rights but a chasm between their respective views of the state; and what is needed to effect a cessation of atrocities is probably the general acceptance not of a theory of rights but of a common view of power and its exercise. I would not presume to explain why the Tudor policy in Ireland was far more ghastly than Gladstonian policy—however benighted the latter might have been—but the answer is not the development of a theory of human *rights*. The most horrible abuses of our world do not seem to end because one side has suddenly come to its jurisprudential or philosophical senses. (Occasionally human rights abuses—apartheid in South Africa would be a recent example—do end for the old-fashioned eighteenth-century reason that people far away come to recognize them as morally exigent.)

One might thus generalize from the first essay as follows: a politics of human rights must observe the constraints Ignatieff has so cogently presented. It must understand—as our predecessors did—the virtue of order over anarchy in all but the most dire circumstances. Hence Ignatieff's stress on respecting state sovereignty and on constitutional guarantees. The international human rights movement ought to support the weak against the strong; the language of human rights is a weapon in that struggle. It should choose its interventions carefully, following certain criteria, and with careful attention to the sufficiency of means to ends. But it is within the spirit of Ignatieff's first essay, I think, to suggest that an international politics in support of individual liberties might look beyond rights to supporting the social and cultural conditions under which neighbors can cease to regard one another as incompatible with civilization and instead return to "what is proper and becoming between people."

NOTES

1. Sir Thomas Elyot, *The Boke named the Governour* (London, 1531), ed. Donald W. Rude (New York and London: Garland Publishing, 1992), bk. 2, chap. 8, p. 138.

2. Carlo Ginzburg, "Killing a Chinese Mandarin: On the Moral Implications of Distance," *Critical Inquiry* 21, no. 1 (Autumn 1994): 46–60.

3. Adam Smith, *Theory of Moral Sentiments*, ed. A. L. Macfie and D. D. Raphael (Oxford: Clarendon Press, 1976), 3 [3.4], 136–37.

4. Primo Levi, *The Drowned and the Saved,* trans. from the Italian by Raymond Rosenthal (New York: Summit Books, 1988), pp. 56–57.

5. Nicolas Malebranche, *The Search after Truth,* trans. and ed. by Thomas M. Lennon and Paul J. Olscamp (Cambridge: Cambridge University Press, 1997), 4:11, 323.

6. William Wollaston, *The Religion of Nature Delineated* (London, 1724; Delmar, N.Y.: Scholars' Facsimiles and Reprints, 1974), 139–40.

7. Smith, *Theory of Moral Sentiments,* 1, [1.1], 9.

8. J. H. Plumb, *The Growth of Political Stability in England: 1675–1725* (Baltimore: Penguin Books, 1969).

9. Hermann Hesse, "The Longing of Our Time for a Worldview," in *The Weimar Republic Sourcebook,* ed. Anton Kaes, Martin Jay, and Edward Dimendberg (Berkeley and Los Angeles: University of California Press, 1994), p. 365.

Relativism and Religion

DIANE F. ORENTLICHER

"HUMAN RIGHTS," Louis Henkin wrote in 1981, "is the idea of our time."[1] But as Michael Ignatieff reminds us, human rights is an idea without an idea—an idea, that is, without a professed ideology. Conspicuously absent from the Universal Declaration of Human Rights is language evoking commitment to a particular belief system, and this was hardly an oversight: After all, the drafters of this instrument hoped to secure universal adherence in a world starkly divided by tradition, religion, and above all ideology.

But as Ignatieff notes, their efforts were never wholly successful, and the final decade of the twentieth century brought a resurgent challenge to the core claim of international human rights law—that *every* person *everywhere* is entitled to certain rights by virtue of being human. I am referring, of course, to the challenge of cultural relativism.

In what is perhaps its strongest form, the relativist critique can be summarized this way: Moral claims derive their meaning and legitimacy from the (particular) cultural tradition in which they are embedded. What we call "universal" human rights are, in fact, an expression above all of Western values derived from the Enlightenment.

Understood in this light, the human rights idea is at best misguided in its core claim that it embodies universal values—and at worst a blend of moral hubris and cultural imperialism.

The relativist critique presents a powerful intellectual challenge to the idea of human rights. But it is above all a challenge to the *legitimacy* of the human rights movement. Unless countered persuasively, the relativist challenge threatens the effectiveness, and not simply the intellectual coherence, of that movement. With this in mind, a key premise of my commentary is that a successful response to the relativist challenge is one that effectively advances the legitimacy of human rights across diverse cultures.

It may be helpful at the outset to identify several distinct strategies that have been deployed to counter the relativist challenge. I do so in the hope of bringing further clarity to the subject at hand, and not merely providing fresh evidence of the academic's penchant for inventing arcane categories of analysis. For present purposes, four strategies are particularly relevant: (1) substantive accommodation; (2) moral anthropology; (3) procedural inclusiveness; and its close relation, (4) transnational collaboration.

The legitimacy of human rights, I will argue, depends crucially on the last two strategies. And, I will suggest, recognizing the importance of these two strategies may require those of us who address human rights principally from an international perspective to be more open to efforts to legitimize human rights through religious commitments.

SUBSTANTIVE ACCOMMODATION:
IGNATIEFF'S THIN UNIVERSALISM

The most familiar responses to the relativist critique take the form of substantive accommodation. This approach seeks to reconcile the core claim of human rights with the moral implications of cultural diversity by defining the appropriate substantive province of international standards on the one hand and of moral pluralism on the other. An example of this type of response is what Jack Donnelly calls "weak cultural relativism," an approach that recognizes a comprehensive set of prima facie universal human rights but permits some measure of local exceptions and variations, the latter primarily through particularized interpretations of universal standards.[2] A similar approach is reflected in case law holding that the European Convention on Human Rights allows Contracting Parties a "margin of appreciation" in interpreting and applying certain provisions of the convention.[3] When applicable, this doctrine legitimizes local variations in the interpretation and application of obligations imposed by the convention, which establishes a regional analogue to universal standards.

A claim that takes the form of substantive accommodation lies at the heart of Ignatieff's elegant and richly textured response to the relativist challenge: The universal claims of human rights instruments are and must remain "self-consciously minimalist." Their aim should be to protect human agency—not to legislate moral, political, or cultural conformity.

This approach is compelling in large measure because it is deeply principled: Ignatieff's vision is informed above all by values that are central to the contemporary law of human rights. While asserting a universal entitlement, the idea of human rights demands that we honor our common humanity by respecting human agency—and that means leaving wide scope for pluralism in the way we define and pursue the good life.

But however appealing, this account cannot by itself offer a complete response to the relativist challenge. Like any version of substantive accommodation, Ignatieff's account raises—and, if it is to persuade, must be able to answer—the question, By whose lights does one determine which rights are, in Donnelly's terms, *"prima facie* universal"* and what local variations in interpretation are permissible? If adherents to Islam in a particular culture believe that amputations undertaken pursuant to judicial determination do not constitute torture, does their claim fall within Donnelly's zone of permissible local variation in the interpretation of norms that are universal (in this case, the prohibition of torture)? Or do such amputations violate a norm that is not subject to local exceptions or variations in interpretation? *Who decides?*

Ignatieff suggests that there is no real dilemma if universal rights claims remain minimalist. As long as the human rights agenda is confined to protecting rights necessary to secure individual agency, it will have done its work. But the example he invokes—efforts to address genital mutilation—proves just how vexing this project can be. "What may appear as mutilation in Western eyes," Ignatieff begins, "is simply the price of tribal and family belonging to women." Provided certain preconditions exist—here Ignatieff invokes the medical model of informed consent—Western activists must accept that "it is for women themselves to decide how to make the adjudication between tribal and Western wisdom." The challenge is "to create conditions in which individuals on the bottom are free to avail themselves of such rights as they want." But what does this mean if not that human rights advocates should try to transform core values of communities in which genital mutilation is practiced? Ignatieff sees the problem, and ultimately concludes that such practices "can be abandoned only when the whole community decides to do so. Otherwise, individuals who decide on their own face ostracism and worse. Consent in these cases means collective or group consent."

More fundamentally (and of special pertinence to Ignatieff's position), the strongest version of cultural relativism challenges the universality of rights on the asserted ground that the core concept of individual rights has no foundation, or at any rate is not deeply rooted, in many cultural traditions.

Ignatieff is keenly aware of this challenge and offers a sophisticated, multilayered response. Against the claim that human rights are Western values masquerading as universal norms, he reminds us that legions of individuals across diverse cultures have embraced the individual rights paradigm embodied in postwar human rights law. Indeed, he argues, "it is precisely this individualism that renders [the language of rights] attractive to non-Western peoples and explains why human rights has become a global movement."

When it comes to human rights, Ignatieff asserts, universality cannot mean that every sentient person must buy into the idea. In particular, we can scarcely expect to persuade "holders of power of the universal validity of rights doctrines, since if these doctrines prevailed, they would necessarily abridge and constrain their exercise of authority." What matters is that "the people who are making [claims to rights protection] are . . . the victims themselves."

This argument will sound familiar to those who have followed the human rights movement in recent years. Confronted with challenges to the legitimacy of their own efforts, leaders of international human rights organizations are quick to note that authoritarian leaders cynically invoke the charge of cultural imperialism to deflect criticism from abroad. Bolstering their defense, international advocates cite their collaboration with local activists as evidence that they are not attempting to foist Western values upon societies with profoundly different cultures.

Their defense has powerful appeal—but mainly for those already committed to human rights. As a response to the relativist challenge, it begs fundamental questions. In many of the "non-Western" societies evoked by Ignatieff, individuals who lay claim to the protection of global human rights constitute a distinct minority. What, then, do their views tell us about the extent to which the human rights idea enjoys universal acceptance? Across many societies a broad swath of humanity has not embraced even the minimalist human rights paradigm endorsed by Ignatieff—and their ranks are scarcely composed solely of cynical despots. Thus, without a principled basis for crediting the views of believers as against those of nonbelievers, we may be left with the bare claim that human rights are universal because those who support the idea support the idea.[4]

Moral Anthropology: A Prudential Humanism

If we cannot establish the universal legitimacy of human rights merely by counting hands, how should we judge its claim to universality? Is there a justifying idea behind human rights after all—an idea that imports its own claim of universality?

Ignatieff rightly regards this question as central. "Why do human beings have rights in the first place?" he asks. "What is it about the human species and the human individual that entitles them to rights?" That the answers remain elusive more than half a century into the international human rights movement accounts at least in part for what Ignatieff calls a "spiritual crisis" for adherents to the secular faith of human rights.

It is tempting to seek large answers for questions that concern the deepest interests of humanity. Yet it is precisely this temptation we must resist, Ignatieff argues. His reasons are complex, both principled and pragmatic. To begin, Ignatieff believes that we imperil the consensus underlying his minimalist human rights project if we move onto the contested ground of foundational claims. The "deliberate silence at the heart of human rights culture" is precisely what makes it possible to sustain universal belief in its core claims.[5]

More important to Ignatieff's argument are the perils captured in the metaphor of idolatry. Heeding the warning of Exodus, secular humanists, like religious believers, must take care lest a worshipful faith in human sanctity blind them to their own capacity for fallibility. Even a secular humanism is susceptible to harmful immoderation if unchecked by critical self-scrutiny.

For Ignatieff, then, the risks of idolatry are not confined to religious justifications for human rights. But he seems especially leery of religiously grounded claims. Ignatieff has little trouble rounding up historical evidence in support of his fear that religious zealotry, far from serving to protect human rights, may lead to much the opposite result. Still, this seems less an argument against a faith-based commitment to human rights than a brief against religious intolerance—unless one believes the first leads inexorably to the second.[6]

Ignatieff is understandably suspicious of some writers' claims that their own religious commitments provide the most secure foundation for "universal" human rights. But not all efforts to justify human rights in religious terms evoke the troubling specter that Ignatieff has conjured. His concerns seem misplaced, for example, when it comes to the claims of Michael Perry, which Ignatieff cites disapprovingly. It is difficult to find warrant in Perry's views for Ignatieff's general claim that "the religious side believes that only if humans get down on their knees can they save themselves from their own destructiveness." In fact, Perry's core claim—that the idea of human rights is "ineliminably religious"—is not so far afield from Ignatieff's own views. For Perry, to say that the idea of human rights is "ineliminably religious" means that it rests on the belief that every person is sacred.[7] Compare this to Ignatieff's concession that, although "humanists do not literally worship human rights, . . . we use the language to say that there is something inviolate about the dignity of each human being."

In this, Ignatieff discerns the same risk of "cultlike credulity" against which he has cautioned. If humanists wish to be consistent, Ignatieff concludes, they must concede "that there *is* nothing sacred about human beings, nothing entitled to worship or ultimate respect." But if there is nothing about human beings that entitles them to ultimate respect, what can justify the belief—Ignatieff's belief—"that human beings are not free to do what they wish with other human beings; that human beings should not be beaten, tortured, coerced, indoctrinated, or in any way sacrificed against their will"?

Ignatieff tackles this question through a fundamentally prudential strategy I have termed moral anthropology in defense of what he calls secular humanism. Our basic intuitions that human beings may not inflict abominations on others derive, Ignatieff says, "from our own experience of pain and our capacity to imagine the pain of others." And, he says: "All that can be said about human rights is that they are necessary to protect individuals from violence and abuse, and if it is asked why, the only possible answer is historical." The basic justification for human rights, then, comes down to a deep intuition, reinforced by ghastly experience, that human beings should not be slaughtered wholesale, coupled with the conviction that an individual-rights paradigm is the best available bulwark against this specter.

Ignatieff fairly describes the intuitions and experiences that have driven the human rights movement. But this is not an account that goes far in addressing the concerns of those who doubt the legitimacy of human rights. Ignatieff knows this and makes clear that he does not expect his arguments to convert nonbelievers. This, at any rate, seems implicit in his observation that "[i]t would be a hopeless task to attempt to persuade . . .

holders of power of the universal validity of rights doctrines."

But it is not just "holders of power" who challenge the universality of rights. In fact, the charge of cultural imperialism falls easily from the lips of authoritarian leaders precisely because they know it has broad resonance. To insist that "[r]elativism is the invariable alibi of tyranny" is to silence countless individuals who have a deeper commitment to the values they have cherished for a lifetime than to universal rights drafted a world away from their experience. If the despot's charge of cultural imperialism is to be countered effectively, the relativist critique must be taken seriously on its own terms.

How effectively we meet that challenge is deeply consequential, for even Ignatieff's modest human rights agenda makes radical claims on societies—claims we can hardly expect societies to meet if they doubt, or even reject outright, the legitimacy of human rights. Consider, for example, the prohibition of torture, which appears on every short list of truly universal standards. It has long been recognized that, to make the prohibition effective, states must adopt rather sophisticated legal regimes and, usually, reforms. Thus long after international law proscribed torture, the United Nations adopted a treaty specifying legal measures that must be taken to ensure its eradication.[8] The implications of those undertakings became clear when they served as the basis for the determination by British Law Lords that General Augusto Pinochet could be extradited to Spain to stand trial on allegations of torture. This ruling shattered long-settled expectations even among Western countries with an established tradition of respect for the rule of law. In societies lacking such a tradition, the Torture Convention would require major institutional changes, which cannot occur without a corresponding transformation in these societies' legal and political cultures.

The point here is that even seemingly straightforward universal norms like the prohibition of torture may require societies to undertake profound transformations. And this can happen only where human rights enjoys both deep and broad legitimacy.

PROCEDURAL INCLUSIVENESS

The approach I call procedural inclusiveness goes some way toward addressing this concern. This strategy recognizes that the human rights idea faces a crisis of legitimacy principally because the *process* by which key international treaties were drafted was highly exclusionary. With this diagnosis, the cure suggests itself: the transcultural process by which "universal" rights are constructed must become truly inclusive. And as Ignatieff suggests, we must be committed to the ideal of an "intercultural dialogue in which all parties come to the table under common expectations of being treated as moral equals."

In some versions, strategies that fall under the rubric of procedural inclusiveness respond directly to the relativist challenge. The basic argument can be briefly stated: All values are social constructs. As such, they reflect the particular sociocultural tradition or traditions from which they derive. This is as true for universal human rights as for values derived from a manifestly particularistic tradition, such as the rules governing purification observed by traditional Romani communities. Historically, the project of constructing universal human rights has been highly exclusionary; the postwar body of law was, after all, constructed at a time when many of today's states could not participate in the norm-setting process because they were still colonized. Still, to recognize this is not to condemn wholesale the project of seeking to construct a universal code of humanity. What is needed, instead, is a process that is more nearly universal. At stake is the global legitimacy of human rights. For, as Amy Gutmann and Dennis Thompson have observed, the moral authority of collective judgments depends in part upon the moral quality of the process by which those judgments are reached.[9]

It is, of course, easier to describe than to realize the ideal of a truly universal process of constructing, reconstructing, and refining universal human rights. Unless one has participated in an international conference convened to draft a new human rights instrument, one cannot fully appreciate how profoundly the outcome of such a drafting process is determined by the skewed distribution of political power and resources among representatives of states that have ostensibly equal votes. That all states can now claim a seat at the proverbial table when international instruments are drafted is, to be sure, an important advance since the postwar period. But if every state is entitled to contribute its perspectives to the intercultural process of constructing universal norms, this scarcely assures that every voice will have an equal opportunity to be heard.[10]

These imbalances compound the already daunting challenges inherent in an intercultural project of constructing norms that will enjoy deep legitimacy across diverse moral traditions—traditions whose basic perspectives may be largely incommensurate. Still, we are more likely to approach Ignatieff's ideal dialogue, in which all participants have common expectations of being treated as moral equals, if we confront that challenge with an acute awareness of how profoundly our perspectives—the very way that we apprehend such concepts as "universality" and "rights"—are shaped and limited by our own intellectual and cultural traditions.

TRANSNATIONAL COLLABORATION

Closely related to procedural inclusiveness is the strategy of transnational collaboration. While procedural inclusiveness is concerned with the process by which human rights standards are defined, transnational collaboration focuses on strategies of cooperation in securing compliance with those norms. Transnational collaboration is critical both in securing states' compliance with human rights norms and in consolidating the legitimacy of the norms themselves in a multicultural world.

The latter point has been highlighted by the controversy surrounding efforts to eradicate female genital mutilation. The most trenchant criticism of global campaigns against this practice has focused on the culturally insensitive strategies employed by many Western feminists rather than on their substantive claims. As this controversy has made clear, strategies aimed at enforcing human rights claims can have a crucial effect in establishing the transcultural legitimacy of the norms themselves.

In larger perspective, strategies emphasizing transnational collaboration recognize that the force behind enforcement of human rights has come principally from individuals and other nonstate actors—and that the power of their efforts is amplified by transnational collaboration. This is, of course, a phenomenon that Ignatieff's writing has illuminated with singular clarity. Notable instances include the transnational collaboration among human rights advocates that led to the initiation of criminal proceedings against former Chilean president Augusto Pinochet in Spain and in other Western European countries and against former Chadian president Hissène Habré in Senegal.

A striking feature of transnational collaboration among nonstate actors is the dynamic process of cross-cultural dialogue that ensues (at least sometimes) among the collaborators. In the course of cooperating to secure enforcement of international law, transnational coalitions have been constructing, to use Michael Ignatieff's words, "a genuinely global human rights culture."[11]

ENGAGING RELIGION

It is particularly with such nonstate actors in mind that I return to one of the more vexing issues raised by Ignatieff: How should we regard contemporary efforts to ground human rights in religious terms? In addressing this question, I believe that a primary focus of our concern should be nonstate actors who seek to transform their own societies' legal institutions and political cultures in light of human rights ideals—not the authoritarian leader who cynically charges "cultural imperialism" to deflect the scrutiny of global conscience.

Although Ignatieff believes that the principal task of human rights is to create a protected zone of autonomy in which each of us can define our own meaning of the good life, he seemingly prefers that we find that meaning largely outside the idea of human rights itself—especially when our definition of the good life is fundamentally religious in nature. His views on this are perplexing, for they seem at odds with one of his core claims. Ignatieff believes that the "fundamental moral commitment entailed by rights is . . . to deliberation," which requires at a minimum "a willingness to remain in the same room, listening to claims one doesn't like to hear." Yet Ignatieff believes it is best "to forgo . . . altogether" debate about claims that ground human rights in religious or other ultimate terms. Here, he seems confident, reasoned deliberation cannot serve its purpose.

I wonder, too, whether Ignatieff's wary response to those who seek justification for human rights in religion takes adequate account of a crucial fact: universal acceptance of the human rights idea depends upon its legitimation *within* diverse religious traditions, and not just *alongside* them. In the near term, for example, it is difficult to imagine further progress—and here I mean human rights progress—in Iran that is not rooted in and justified by reformist clerics' progressive interpretation of Islam.

As Abdullahi An-Na'im has argued, "international human rights norms are unlikely to be accepted by governments . . . and respected in practice, without strong legitimation within national politics," and this includes broad acceptance of human rights norms as being at least consistent with the religious beliefs of the population.[12] This may, and often does, require adherents to diverse religions to reinterpret some of the precepts of their religions in light of international human rights standards. The idea of human rights is revolutionary not just because it challenges state power, as has so often been noted, but also because it often requires transformation of fundamental belief systems. For this reason I am inclined to share An-Na'im's belief that human rights advocates would do well "to seriously engage religion"[13] rather than seek to exclude religious discourse from the intercultural process of constructing and construing human rights.

This type of engagement need not heighten the risks of idolatry against which Ignatieff cautions vigilance. To be willing genuinely to engage disparate perspectives should not be confused with undertaking to find a common consensus on the metaphysics of rights at the end of the dialogue. Rather, Ignatieff gets the point precisely right when he implores us "to respect the reasoned commitments of others," to commit ourselves "to remain in the same room" when confronted with "claims one doesn't like to hear."

Nor is it apparent why a more skeptical approach might be warranted when the "claims one doesn't like to hear" are religious. As Michael Perry has argued, to accept the proposition that the idea of human rights is "ineliminably religious" does not require a commitment to any *particular* religion.[14] Much less, then, does a willingness genuinely to engage religion in the ongoing dialogue that defines the human rights movement entail a surrender of commitment to pluralism or a greater tendency toward idolatrous zeal. Indeed, greater engagement of religion—or, more to the point, of plural religious perspectives—by human rights advocates would surely enhance the type of cross-cultural dialogue that operates as a check against absolutism.

More important, such engagement may be necessary if the idea of human rights is to take root within the deepest commitments of individuals across diverse systems of belief, tradition, and culture. To paraphrase Ignatieff, human rights cannot go truly global unless it goes deeply local. Only when this happens can the idea of human rights achieve its radically transformative aims.

Notes

I am grateful to Abdullahi A. An-Na'im, M. Gregg Bloche, and Michael J. Perry for comments on earlier drafts and to Donald Viera for research assistance.

1. Louis Henkin, introduction to *The International Bill of Rights: The Covenant on Civil and Political Rights,* ed. Louis Henkin (New York: Columbia University Press, 1981).

2. See, e.g., Jack Donnelly, "Cultural Relativism and Universal Human Rights," *Human Rights Quarterly* 6 (1984): 401.

3. While my commentary focuses on the moral implications of the relativist critique, the case law to which I have referred tends to emphasize concerns relating to the enduring prerogatives of state sovereignty in a supranational legal system.

4. Ignatieff himself does not make such a simplistic claim. As noted, he believes that the legitimacy of rights claims "depends entirely on the fact that the people who are making them are the victims themselves."

5. This argument is similar to Cass Sunstein's claim that public judgments on some matters of profound social consequence are best left "incompletely theorized." Sunstein explains that most of the virtues associated with incompletely theorized judgments "involve *the constructive use of silence,* an exceedingly important social and legal phenomenon. Silence—on something that may prove false, obtuse, or excessively contentious—can help minimize conflict, allow the present to learn from the future, and save a great deal of time and expense." Cass R. Sunstein, *Agreement without The-*

ory, in *Deliberative Politics: Essays on Democracy and Disagreement*, ed. Stephen Macedo, pp. 123–50, at 130 (New York: Oxford University Press, 1999) (emphasis in original).

6. Ignatieff does not seem to believe that it does. This seems implicit in his observation that "[r]eligious persons aware of the dangers of idolatry scrutinize their worship for signs of pride, zeal, or intolerance toward other believers."

7. See generally Michael J. Perry, *The Idea of Human Rights: Four Inquiries* (New York: Oxford University Press, 1998).

8. *Convention Against Torture and Other Cruel, Inhuman or Degrading Treatment or Punishment*, Feb. 4, 1985, 39 U.N. GAOR Supp. (No. 51) at 197, U.N. Doc. A/39/41 (1984) (entered into force June 26, 1987) [hereinafter "Torture Convention"].

9. Amy Gutmann and Dennis Thompson, *Democracy and Disagreement* (Cambridge: Harvard University Press, Belknap Press, 1996), p. 4.

10. I want to emphasize that I am not urging a radical version of cultural relativism. That is, I am not suggesting that every perspective is equally valid. My emphasis is on equality of opportunity to have one's perspective taken seriously in the project of constructing international norms.

11. See Michael Ignatieff, "Human Rights: The Midlife Crisis," *New York Review of Books*, May 20, 1999.

12. Abdullahi A. An-Na'im, "Islam and Human Rights: Beyond the Universality Debate" (paper presented at Annual Meeting, American Society of International Law, Washington, D.C., April 6, 2000), p. 4.

13. Ibid., p. 1.

14. Here, it may be helpful to note that, for purposes of his argument, Professor Perry broadly defines a "religious" worldview as one that is "grounded or embedded in a vision of the finally or ultimately meaningful nature of the world and of our place in it" (*The Idea of Human Rights*, p. 15). In his view, "[t]o say that a conviction is 'religious' . . . is to say that the conviction is embedded in a religious vision or cosmology, that it is an aspect, a constituent, of such a vision: a vision according to which the world is ultimately meaningful (in a way hospitable to our deepest yearnings)" (p. 16).

RESPONSE TO
COMMENTATORS

MICHAEL IGNATIEFF

Dignity and Agency

Tom Laqueur takes issue with the degree to which I associate moral progress with the development of human rights. Such progress has occurred, he concedes, but international human rights has not had much to do with it. The decisive factor in the gradual reduction of cruelty and unmerited suffering in the Western world, he argues, has been not the growth of transnational rights instruments but the creation of regimes of constitutional law and political stability in Europe and the North Atlantic world since the sixteenth century. This struggle for political stability created the domestic rights regimes, which gradually ended the exercise of arbitrary power in the European and North Atlantic worlds. Here what proved crucial to moral progress was the emergence of an idea of political community in which citizens could count on immunity from arbitrary arrest and rights of free speech and assembly. The slow consolidation of Western citizenship took violence out of Western politics and engendered new conceptions of solidarity among strangers, conceived anew as a community of citizens. Moral solidarity—and moral progress—are thus linked historically to the creation of modern democratic political cultures. These are the cultures where rights are strong and afford genuine protection. Beyond the boundaries of these states, rights culture remains weak to this day.

Over the same historical period that internal rights regimes were being consolidated within the borders of European and North Atlantic states, Laqueur argues, European peoples were rethinking their moral connections to strangers beyond their borders. Here Laqueur argues that the decisive influences in the early transnational moral campaigns like antislavery were the twin forces of Christian ethics and moral sympathy confronting the globalizing industry of their time, namely, the slave trade. Natural rights arguments, he implies, were much less important in generating the campaign to end the trade than what Adam Smith and other psychologists of the Enlightenment called the imagination, and we might call "empathy." "Are we not brothers?" was the famous rallying cry of the antislavery movement of the 1780s, rather than "Are we not rights-bearers?"

These historical points lead Laqueur to two important conclusions. The first is that the only really effective rights regimes are "local" ones, anchored in the traditions, institutions, and historical memory of national communities. The second is that in generating links of transnational solidarity beyond these national communities, human rights is a poor substitute for empathy or sympathy, a poor second best to more impalpable conceptions of what is "proper and becoming between people." When human beings lack this civilized sense of what is proper and becoming, when they fail to develop a sense of empathy toward the predicaments of strangers, human rights doctrines alone can do little or nothing to call them back to their better nature.

I do not disagree with the first point—that rights become effective only when they are anchored in the constitutional traditions of particular peoples. Nor do I disagree with the second point that effective transnational solidarity must draw on deeper vocabularies of moral concern than rights. Without the moral imagination to feel the pain of others as if it were your own, there cannot be any solidarity worth the name. And if, as Diane Orentlicher adds, a sense that human beings are sacred has helped to sustain the transnational commitments of religious people, human rights activists should not let a doctrinal secularism stand in the way of their collaborating with them and fully respecting their commitments. But there is a third implication of Tom Laqueur's argument that seems to misunderstand what is new about human rights. He writes as if human rights were just a juridical articulation of duty by those in zones of safety toward those in zones of danger, as if modern international human rights were just the attenuated secular form of Christian duty as expressed in the antislavery campaign. This would be to miss what has been historically new about international human rights: the way that they empower victims and validate their entitlement to freedom. Antislavery activists in the eighteenth century conceived of slaves as brothers all right, but also as dependents in tutelage. Modern international human rights conceives of victims as rights-bearers, empowered to protect themselves—with our help, if possible, but by their own means, if necessary. This is what I mean when I say that human rights has gone global, by going local. Because victims are conceived as rights-bearing equals, rather than the dependent beneficiaries of our moral concern, human rights language commands those who can give help to treat those who seek it as equals and to respect them as independent agents.

My argument that human rights are essentially designed to validate and enhance human agency depends, it must be confessed, upon a culturally relative idea of human dignity and worth. It is best to confess this since the essays themselves sought to do without the idea of dignity at all. I now see the force of both Anthony Appiah's and Diane Orentlicher's belief that you cannot do without some notion of intrinsic dignity to sustain belief in human rights. Appiah thinks, "[O]rdinary people almost everywhere have something like the notion of dignity." Diane Orentlicher wonders how anyone can ground a duty not to torture or abuse other human beings unless there is some primary notion that human beings are entitled to "ultimate respect."

While I concede this point, I still have a difficulty about dignity. There are many forms and expressions of human dignity, and some of them strike me as profoundly inhumane. Rituals of sexual initiation, like genital cutting, for example, are linked to an idea of womanly dignity and worth. Likewise, ultra-Orthodox Judaism imposes a role on women that secular women find oppressive, but that religious women find both fulfilling and respectful of their dignity. So ideas of dignity that are supposed to unite different cultures in some shared attachment to human rights actually divide us. There is no easy way round the culturally specific and relative character of the idea of dignity. My suggestion was to link dignity to agency, on the assumption that cultures could then agree that what matters is the right of people to construe dignity as they wish, not the content they give to it. Dignity as agency is thus the most plural, the most open definition of the word I can think of. Still, I cannot escape the fact that connecting dignity to free agency is more plausible in some cultures than in others. The idea of dignity implicit in human rights texts is mostly taken from the classical European ideal of republican citizenship, from the political conception of human beings as entitled to participate in the making of the laws that rule them, to deliberate freely over their meaning, and to be protected from the arbitrary exercise of power. In this conception, human dignity expresses itself in political and civil freedom, in the exercise of individual choice and collective deliberation. In effect, international human rights covenants and declarations seek to re-create for the international society of states the norms that govern the relation between citizen and state in a democratic polity, to make all human beings citizens rather than subjects of the states they give obedience to.

People from non-Western traditions may not recognize this as dignity, though they might concede, if pressed, that it is hard to think of dignity without some idea of freedom, without some idea of choice and agency. Ironically, it is often those who are deprived of their liberty, slaves and prisoners, who remind us best of the connection between dignity and freedom. They refuse to surrender the tiny margin of autonomy that is left them, and they use it to assert their unvanquished sense of self. There is thus a chain of association that connects together the idea of dignity with the idea of freedom, and both in turn with the capability to maintain and express personal identity.

This connection between personal identity and dignity may strike some as too Western, and too individualistic. In many societies the identity that individuals seem to express is not so much a personal one as the identity of the tribe or group or faith with which the individual associates. But even here, where agency is used to express an identity that is primarily social, the dignity expressed remains the dignity of the individual who expresses it. There seems no way around the individuality of dignity, however socially defined it may be. To express a secondhand identity, one that is not articulated as your own, is to be undignified. So the same chain of association that connects dignity, freedom, and identity links all three to individuality. This chain of associations may be Western in origin, but origins do not determine applicability, and the applicability of human rights, its popularity beyond the West, seems to depend on the capacity of the language to conjure up the dream of a dignified individual identity for people whose own cultures did not permit such dreams.

There is no way around the individualism implicit in this idea of dignity, and instead of apologizing for individualism as a bias, we need to stress its advantages. These become evident when a human rights perspective is added to theories and strategies of economic development. As Amartya Sen and others have shown, a human rights perspective, focusing as it does on enhancing human agency, draws attention to the importance of unblocking individual agency as a motor for economic development itself. Human rights, like freedom of speech and assembly, as well as freedom of the press, are essential in creating checks and balances against coercive development strategies by governments. A free society is unlikely to make the costly and unjust development choices that an unfree society will, simply because freedom creates feedback mechanisms that channel discontent upward to elites and force them to abandon ill-conceived or unwise policies. Moreover, a rights perspective tests development programs and policies by whether they actually benefit individuals. A human rights perspective on development, for example, would be critical of any macroeconomic strategy that purchased aggregate economic growth at the price of the rights of significant groups of individuals. A dam project that boosts electro-generation capacity at the price of flooding the lands of poor people without compensation and redress is an injustice, even if the aggregate economic benefit of such a measure is clear.

If the advantages of the individualistic bias in human rights are clear, it must also be said that human rights can do a lot more than protect individuals. As Anthony Appiah's discussion of group rights and membership rights shows, the agency that human rights is often trying to defend is the agency of collectivities, which are thereby enabled to safeguard and enhance the cultures, capabilities, and languages of the individuals who constitute them. Protecting individuals while also protecting groups is not easy. Appiah is clear—as am I—that when you have to choose, individual rights should prevail over group ones, since the very purpose of a group would be frustrated if it suppressed the rights and claims of the individuals who compose it.

Historically, most Western rights regimes have been hostile to group rights and membership rights, believing that rights should confer one single, solitary belonging, to the national community. Yet this solitary belonging to a single national community can be hard on minorities. They secure incorporation into the national rights community at the price of being forced to give up what is distinctive to their collective identity. Once upon a time, Breton peasants could be forced into becoming Frenchmen, through the rigors of the public education system of France's Third Republic, but nowadays, and thanks mostly to the spread of ideas of rights to self-determination and autonomy, most minorities refuse to pay the price of forcible assimilation into national cultures. Aboriginal peoples, linguistic and religious minorities have used the language of rights to secure collective entitlement to preserve their heritages. The result is that most modern national communities do not maintain one single set of equal rights for all. They also simultaneously maintain minority rights regimes to language, land, and religious practice. So there is no real sense in which individual rights are reductive of cultural difference. Indeed, rights regimes, within nation-states, have become the chief bulwark for the protection of cultural, religious, and social pluralism. If anything, the chief contemporary criticism of rights talk is that, by enfranchising and protecting so many minorities, rights fragment citizenship and national belonging. Yet there is no reason in principle why citizens cannot enjoy two types of rights at once—those that they enjoy with all other citizens, and those that they enjoy by virtue of their particular minority status.

Reconciling group rights and national belonging is possible when national cultures are strong and cohesive, and rights themselves find secure anchorage in deeply felt national traditions. When rights are anchored in tradition, adjudication of rights claims becomes easier because disputants feel obliged, by the weight of these traditions, to abide by the results of adjudication. Exporting rights traditions to non-Western societies—the chief burden of postwar international human rights—is a much more problematic exercise.

If human rights is about protecting and enhancing human dignity, defined as the capacity to be a free agent, what right do we in the West have to advocate a notion of dignity that is so inimical to the way dignity is defined, especially for women, in most of the world's cultures? My approach to this problem in the essays was to argue that free agency is not such a strange or Eurocentric idea after all. Judging from the demand, especially by women, for emancipation from the tutelage and oppression of traditional society, we can say that free agency is a popular idea, and we in the West should be less apologetic about promoting it. Diane Orentlicher is critical of this approach, correctly observing that just because an idea is popular does not make it universal. The fact that human rights has gone global by going local, that is, by sustaining local demands by ordinary people for some exercise of free agency, does not really prove that the idea of dignity as agency is genuinely universal. David Hollinger goes further and pointedly asks whom I am trying to persuade. Why should patriarchal, theocratic authoritarians want to have anything to do with dignity as agency?

The very idea challenges their power, and no amount

of persuasion on my part is going to bring them over to my side. In an important sense, I am not trying to persuade them. Human rights are a political set of claims that seek to enhance and defend the powerless against the powerful. By definition, patriarchal, theocratic authoritarians are not going to sign up.

Still, as Orentlicher argues, it will not do simply to put resistance to human rights down to the interests of the powerful. Even those who have no power interests to defend may find aspects of human rights norms hard to reconcile with their cultures and traditions. How are these cultural disputes to be negotiated in such a way that cross-cultural support for human rights is strengthened rather than weakened? All of her suggestions here are extremely helpful. She follows my own argument in insisting that human rights proponents are under an obligation, intrinsic to the idea of respecting the agency of others, not to impose their values, but to seek, wherever possible, to negotiate forms of intercultural understanding of what human rights norms entail in particular situations. Each culture ought to have a significant "margin of appreciation" in the manner in which it interprets universal human rights norms, and as she says, the norms of human rights themselves require that the process of discussion across cultures about how wide this margin should be must follow norms of "procedural inclusiveness." That is exactly what I meant when I said that the idea of dignity as agency commits us, not to the idea that individuals are sacred, but to the proposition that individuals are deliberative equals whose views are entitled to a respectful hearing in all moral discussions about how universal standards should apply in each instance. The idea

of dignity as agency entails an ideal of deliberative equality. You cannot impose human rights values: they will not
take hold if you do. Besides, imposition violates the very
principles you are seeking to uphold. So the margins of
appreciation open to each culture are going to be large,
and outsiders to the culture will have to learn to live with
a lot that may seem illiberal or inhumane to them, but
which continues to receive the support of the indigenous
culture.

This is what David Hollinger calls my "strategic minimalism." Define the goal of human rights as enhancing
and protecting human agency. Forestall liberal imperialism by building in safeguards of "procedural inclusiveness." Let the locals define the agenda. For Hollinger,
this is liberal tolerance in a typically equivocal disguise.
The patriarchal, theocratic authoritarians will not be
fooled. They know that human rights are a dagger aimed
at their power. So why not just come out and say what I
really want, which is a world in the image of liberal
democracy?

I could say this, of course, but I would have to face up
to the fact that the establishment of constitutional democracy worldwide is a distant prospect indeed. Those
who do the counting tell us that there are more function-
ing democracies in the world today than at any point in
history. But there is no happy fatality to history, nothing
inevitable or irreversible about the further spread of democracy. The tide can ebb as well as crest. In several
zones of the world—central and West Africa, the south
Caucasus, the Afghan-Pakistan region, and the Indonesian archipelago—state order has either disintegrated altogether or is in the process of fragmenting. For these

zones of the world, democracy is beyond the bounds of expectation. Order will have to come first, and a bloody order it will probably be.

More to the point, there is some doubt whether majoritarian democracy is actually favorable to human rights. When democracy came to Serbia, it brought with it authoritarian populism, restraints on the press, adventurism, and ethnic cleansing. When democracy came to Indonesia, it may have brought with it (we do not know how the story will turn out) the eventual disintegration of the state. So there is a problem with whether liberal values—human rights and democracy—actually entail or in fact contradict one another. It cannot be said that the converse is true—that suppression of democracy is good for human rights—but it also cannot be said with confidence that the advent of democracy improves the human rights of those who do not happen to belong to the electoral majority.

Moreover, and this comes back to a point made by Tom Laqueur, political legitimacy is always local: power translates itself into legitimate authority by exploiting and using the traditions and symbols of the local political culture. In many parts of the world, both democracy and constitutional liberalism are alien to the local political culture, and there is little chance in the short and medium term to change that fact. And if bringing democracy means risking civil war and the disintegration of the state, then the risk, in human rights terms, may not be worth running.

All of this leads me to think that majoritarian democracy is, in many societies, a distant goal, and even an undesirable one, if achieved at the cost of order and human rights. So if this is true, what should our goals as believers in human rights be? Here my slogan would be the title of the justly famous essay by my old teacher, Judith Shklar, "Putting Cruelty First."[1] We may not be able to create democracies or constitutions. Liberal freedom may be some way off. But we could do more than we do to stop unmerited suffering and gross physical cruelty. That I take to be the elemental priority of all human rights activism: to stop torture, beatings, killings, rape, and assault and to improve, as best we can, the security of ordinary people. My minimalism is not strategic at all. It is the most we can hope for.

NOTE

1. Judith Shklar, *Ordinary Vices* (Cambridge: Harvard University Press, 1984).

CONTRIBUTORS

K. Anthony Appiah, Charles H. Carswell Professor of Afro-American Studies and of Philosophy at Harvard University, is the author of *Color Conscious: The Political Morality of Race* (with Amy Gutmann) and coeditor (with Henry Louis Gates Jr.) of *The Dictionary of Global Culture* and the CD-ROM *Encarta Africana*.

Amy Gutmann, Laurance S. Rockefeller University Professor of Politics at Princeton University, is the author of *Color Conscious* (with K. Anthony Appiah), *Democracy and Disagreement* (with Dennis Thompson), and most recently a new edition of *Democratic Education*.

David A. Hollinger, Chancellor's Professor of History at the University of California at Berkeley, is the author of *Science, Jews, and Secular Culture: Studies in Mid-Twentieth-Century American Intellectual History*, and *Postethnic America: Beyond Multiculturalism*.

Michael Ignatieff, writer, historian, broadcaster, is currently the Director of The Carr Center for Human Rights Policy at The Kennedy School of Government, Harvard University. He is the author of *Virtual War: Kosovo and Beyond* and *Isaiah Berlin: A Life*, among others.

Thomas W. Laqueur, Professor of History at the University of California at Berkeley, is the author of *Making Sex: Body and Gender from the Greeks to Freud*.

DIANE F. ORENTLICHER, Professor of Law and Director of the War Crimes Research Office at American University, is coeditor of *Human Rights*, with Louis Henkin, Gerald L. Neuman, and David W. Leebron.

INDEX

[handwritten: If you thought leg had more self determination → stability]

[handwritten left margin: all states ↕ that respect HR; only minimal degree of freedom of exp. is necessary; You only get sd when you get it]

[handwritten bottom: stability/justice; 1. Its not just a utility argument that Mill would make. Not a claim you won't be virtuous until you do it on your own]

[Handwritten margin notes:]

Legitimacy
State L when protects the HR

Buch. lists HR.

Ch 2 - of the liberty and thought + discussion

States are L.
L means being able to be SD → protect specific HRs
One of the more controversial HRs

People talk about legitimacy — just states are leg, just states protect individuals

SOV + HR
Stability of HR
HR + Legitimacy
strength of HR
On Liberty –
Free speech

Just + Unjust Wars
P. 94/95
Mill's essay on non-intervention

Stability – monitoring pluralism needed subversion
of rights

stability seems to be at odds w/ justice
(If you can't get justice – go for ⓧ

Why not think rights that are just are in line w/ ⓧ
and stability

Must Stability determines justice.

There is a culture
there. To say if
you don't have
real F.S. hard
To say you're
really self-
determining

is there really stability?
Are they really self determining
(some w/ bad dictator)